The savvy Scot Herrick done after she signs the offer letter. *'I've Landed My Dream JOB—NOW What???' is essential reading for those who have triumphantly made it past unemployment and are determined not to find themselves back there again.*

Alexandra Levit, author of 'New Job, New You' and '#MILLENNIALtweet'

Scot Herrick provides savvy, practical and valuable advice to keep your dream job from turning into a nightmare.

Anita Bruzzese, author of '45 Things You Do To Drive Your Boss Crazy,' a nationally syndicated columnist on the workplace, and an award-winning journalist.

You got your dream job...NOW WHAT? Read this book...follow the instructions inside, and you can take your dream job beyond your wildest dreams. With practical tips on how to be successful in the first 30 days at your dream job, this book is a must read for anyone who wants to take control of their career and make it great!

Phil Gerbyshak, author of '10 Ways to Make it Great!' and professional speaker and social media coach

I really admire the pragmatism that Scot Herrick has brought to 'I've Landed My Dream Job—Now What???.' In the process of deconstructing some of the potential challenges and pitfalls that can make or break the first 30 days of a new role, he gives people real tools and tips to enable them to work on their own terms from day one. For those New Work Pioneers choosing to create livable lives for themselves in the corporate world, this is going to be a really valuable resource, showing them how not just to survive, but thrive.

Christine Livingston, Coach and Founder of 'A Different Kind of Work'

Scot Herrick has written a book where the pages come alive to act as your personal coach, guide, and map to the first 30 days on the job. You will wake up from the dream and be able to do your best to make your dream job a reality by crafting working goals, cruising through administrivia, keeping the end in mind, dancing the meet and greet, and following the playbook for your team. And of course, don't forget, your manager is your most important customer! Study and read this book and you will prevent your dream job from becoming a working nightmare.

David Zinger, M. Ed., Founder of The Employee Engagement Network

As one who appreciates and celebrates ACCOMPLISHMENT in all its forms, I was excited to see Scot Herrick take one of the most critical accomplishments of any professional—landing a new job—and create an easy-to-understand formula for how to navigate the organizational perils of the first month...of any job, industry, profession, or level. This guide should be a must read for anybody who is currently seeking employment or even considering it. If you truly want to 'seize the accomplishment' of your next career step, you need not look further than 'I've Landed My Dream Job—Now What???.'

Timothy Johnson, Chief Accomplishment Officer, Carpe Factum, Inc.

I've Landed My Dream Job—Now What???

How to Achieve Success in the First 30 Days in a New Job

By Scot Herrick

Foreword by Jason Alba

Happy Ab☻ut

20660 Stevens Creek Blvd., Suite 210
Cupertino, CA 95014

First Printing: May 5, 2010
Paperback ISBN: 978-1-60005-168-5 (1-60005-168-5)
Place of Publication: Silicon Valley, California, USA
Paperback Library of Congress Number: 2010924867
eBook ISBN: 978-1-60005-169-2 (1-60005-169-3)

Trademarks

All terms mentioned in this book that are known to be trademarks or service marks have been appropriately capitalized. Neither Happy About®, nor any of its imprints, can attest to the accuracy of this information. Use of a term in this book should not be regarded as affecting the validity of any trademark or service mark.

Warning and Disclaimer

Every effort has been made to make this book as complete and as accurate as possible. The information provided is on an "as is" basis. The author(s), publisher, and their agents assume no responsibility for errors or omissions. Nor do they assume liability or responsibility to any person or entity with respect to any loss or damages arising from the use of information contained herein.

Dedication

To Kate

Acknowledgments

One person cannot complete a book; there are always others who have helped build your experiences and influenced your thinking. Most of what is in this book are career lessons from various people I've shared my corporate experience with and the thinking from the great community of career writers I've encountered since starting CubeRules.com.

Everything in life is a lesson. Whether it has been layoffs, promotions, great wins or crushing losses in the competitive marketplace, they all teach us to get better if we want them to. For all of those experiences, good and bad, I am grateful.

I'd also especially like to thank the Happy About team and their work in making this book a reality. From Mitchell Levy, who helped get this in motion, to Liz Tadman, the wonderful taskmaster who gets the book through the publishing process with ease and the rest of the Happy About team—they make the work easy to do.

Finally, I'd like to thank Jason Alba, CEO of JibberJobber.com and author of 'I'm on LinkedIn—Now What??? (2nd Edition)' who started this genre of books and offered many pointers and help for this one.

A Message from Happy About®

Thank you for your purchase of this Happy About book. It is available online at http://happyabout.com/mydreamjob.php or at other online and physical bookstores.

- Please contact us for quantity discounts at sales@happyabout.info
- If you want to be informed by email of upcoming Happy About® books, please email bookupdate@happyabout.info

Happy About is interested in you if you are an author who would like to submit a non-fiction book proposal or a corporation that would like to have a book written for you. Please contact us by email editorial@happyabout.info or phone (1-408-257-3000).

Other Happy About books available include:

- Blitz the Ladder:
  http://happyabout.info/blitz.php
- 42 Rules™ to Jumpstart Your Professional Success:
  http://happyabout.info/42rules/jumpstartprofessionalservices.php
- I'm on LinkedIn—Now What???:
  http://happyabout.info/linkedinhelp.php
- I'm at a Networking Event—Now What???:
  http://www.happyabout.com/networking-event.php
- I'm in a Job Search—Now What???:
  http://www.happyabout.com/jobsearchnowwhat.php
- Storytelling About Your Brand Online & Offline:
  http://www.happyabout.com/storytelling.php
- #MILLENNIALtweet Book01:
  http://www.happyabout.com/thinkaha/millennialtweet01.php
- #DIVERSITYtweet Book01:
  http://www.happyabout.com/thinkaha/diversitytweet01.php
- #JOBSEARCHtweet Book01:
  http://www.happyabout.com/thinkaha/jobsearchtweet01.php
- Rule #1: Stop Talking!:
  http://happyabout.info/listenerspress/stoptalking.php
- The Successful Introvert:
  http://happyabout.info/thesuccessfulintrovert.php
- They Made It!:
  http://happyabout.info/theymadeit.php

Contents

Foreword by Jason Alba

Congratulations—you get to move on from "job search mode" and start your new job—indeed, your dream job!

This book might be one of the most important things you read over the next few months as you settle into your new role. You were hired for a reason and you are there to succeed!

Fortunately, Scot is a student and master of career management for the working professional, and you now have access to his best advice, guidance and tips. From this book you should learn to never stop networking. This is a book about protocol, communication and relationships. It's a book to help you be effective and prove why you were the right person to hire. Take chances, of course, but Scot shows you how to do this with an understanding of the culture and environment, so that you make the very best of your new opportunity.

Get a red pen or highlighter and faithfully read this book daily—it is more than a guide—it is a handbook full of actionable ideas that will contribute to your success for many years to come.

If you find something you disagree with, that is okay! Make a note of it, send an email to Scot, or leave a comment on his website (www.DreamJobNowWhat.com). Your circumstances, and the culture of your company, might require a different course of action from what

Scot recommends. The important thing is that you critically think about the issues and opportunities to intentionally set your career in the right direction.

I know Scot says this is a book for your first four weeks at your dream job but I hope you keep visiting it as a reference at different stages of your employment. When you have digested it all, pass it on as a gift to someone else who has just landed their dream job.

Good luck!

Jason Alba
CEO, JibberJobber.com
Author, 'I'm on LinkedIn—Now What???' (Second Edition)
http://imonlinkedinnowwhat.com/

1 Now Is Not the Time to Relax

Congratulations on landing your dream job!

After the hard work of researching the job, navigating the interview gauntlet, and negotiating your offer, success arrives in the form of an accepted offer. You get to start your dream job! Finally, you can relax.

Not so much.

The next phase is just as tough as getting the dream job in the first place: you need to show that you can succeed in the job and work with your manager, team, and coworkers. Without initial success—hitting the ground running—all your hard work securing your dream job will come to naught.

The pressure to perform is high. Companies have ravaged their workforces to align their revenues and expenses; they cannot afford to carry someone new in the face of this unrelenting pressure. Every employee needs to perform and, if not, will be let go in favor of many others waiting in the wings to get the job. With the high levels of downsizing in this Great Recession, a new hire focuses a big spotlight on the person—*you!*—hired for the job.

Even worse, the pressure for success doesn't give employers time to wait while you learn the job. Employers won't train you on new job skills; you need to have the right skills when you walk in the door. Nor is there great concern for your career, only on what you can produce to help the company meet its goals while the management teams focus on surviving.

In short, whatever you need to do, you need to do it yourself.

It is at this point that most people fail. Why? Because they passively wait until their manager volunteers information critical to doing the job well. They wait and watch their team instead of actively learning what needs doing. They infer what customers need from the work they perform. They assume that work gets done at this company in just the same way as it did at their previous employer. By the time they figure out that what happens here is different than at the last position, it is too late. They have become branded as a slow learner in the job or, worse, not doing the job right. Unfortunately, that initial assessment requires significant work to overcome, if it is overcome at all. Getting a poor initial assessment often dooms the person in the position and the company where the eventual choice is to simply start over.

The other side of the coin is that you've committed your skills and work to a company, for better or for worse. No matter how hard you research the company, manager, team, and job, the truth of the matter is that until you actually start the work and deal with all the new interactions on the job, you won't know whether the company, job, or manager is the right fit for you. Unless you are actively discovering what the new job is about and the culture that encompasses the work, you extend the time it takes you to decide if the position is right for you.

If it takes you six months to discover your job isn't right for you, it takes that much longer to find a different position that *is* right for you. Plus, while you are working in a job that isn't right for you, your risk of producing poor work is very high. Poor work output in a competitive employment environment is hugely detrimental to finding another job that does fit your skills.

Now that you have your dream job, you have critical decisions to make that have nothing to do with the tasks your manager gives you or the job skills you have. Critical decisions need making on how your manager goes about managing people, so you can fit into that management style. Decisions need making about your coworkers and their levels of competence and skills. Other decisions about the customers of your work need making to ensure that the people most affected by your work are more than satisfied. A clear, relatively unbiased view of your new position needs making to ensure you will succeed in the job and the job gives you what you need to get better at what you do.

Most people don't know how to go about gathering the information they need to integrate themselves into the new culture or, once they have the information, what to do with it. They know they should learn this stuff, but don't know how to go about it.

I've landed my dream job—now what???

That's what this book is all about: showing success in the first 30 days after you start a new job, whether at a new company or at a different position in the same company you work at right now.

This book charts out your first four weeks at a new job and tasks you with learning about all the other success characteristics you need besides completing your work assigned by your manager. It asks you to go above and beyond your work output to proactively learn about your company, manager, coworkers, and customers in a way that integrates you into the culture—or decide that the job isn't right for you. Doing these additional tasks helps you learn faster, team quicker, and succeed sooner.

2 | Endings

Before You Begin, You Must End

When we take a new job, we are transitioning from one position to another. That position could be coming out of college into the workforce in our first "real" job. Or it could be moving from a position in one company to another. Or, it could be moving from one position in a company to a different position in the same company.

A key success factor in doing well in your next position is ending well in the position you are in.

There are many reasons for this. First, leaving a position well leaves a favorable impression of your work with your manager, team, and customers. You should not underestimate the importance of this as most of the jobs you will find in the future will be found through the network of people you are working with today. When you are done with your new position, the people you are leaving behind today could easily be the same people you need recommendations from for an interview—or be in a position to hire you for your next position.

Consequently, leaving the work you have in disarray and just walking out the door or totally slacking off the last days of your job won't endear you to the people you leave behind.

Companies, of course, won't treat you well if they need to get rid of people. It's easy to see that behavior, get a new job, and then feel as though you can just walk out the door with no notice. Take the job and shove it, so to speak.

As tempting as that may be for you, the truth is that people hire people for positions, not companies. Your loyalty in leaving a position shouldn't lie with the company; instead, your loyalty should lie with the people you worked with in your old position. It is these people who will paint your reputation in all of their future positions, for better or worse.

The second reason you want to end well in the position you are in is so that you will not have distractions as you ramp up your work in the new position. Having to constantly clean up work from your old position not only doesn't give you time to work on your new assignments, it makes your new manager wonder what kind of a person was just hired to do the work.

If you are not good at tying up your loose ends from the old position, how confident do you think your manager and coworkers will be that you can finish your work for them?

Third, unless you have worked hard to define what "done" means with your old manager and coworkers, you can't confidently push back on their work requests—nor can your new manager if you are in the same company—if they continually ask you to do stuff from your old job.

Getting to a well defined "done," then, becomes a critical success factor in your new job.

How do we get to "done" in the old job?

The critical factor in the transition is knowing your current inventory of work and when it needs to be delivered in the future. Most of us have a task management tracking system we use every day so we know what to work on next. This task management system needs a thorough review to ensure all of the work has been captured in the system and the due dates for the work are updated and accurate. Too often, we just "know" what to do next. This may work fine in an ongoing work situation, but when you start to transition work, you must objectively know all the work that needs doing. Surprises in this short transition time on your old job are very disturbing to managers and coworkers alike. So get your work out of your head and into your task management system so you can talk with your work inventory already set up.

In addition, this inventory needs sharing with your old manager so that there is agreement as to all the work that needs doing. Once there is agreement on the amount of work in your inventory, you can now negotiate what work you can do in the remaining time and what work will need transitioning to someone else after you have moved on. Note that since you will be working with someone else to transition the work, you won't have as much time as normal to complete work on your own during the transition period. Make sure you factor this in your agreement for what work you will do compared with the work you will transition.

Getting agreement from your manager about what work you will do and what work will transition sets you up to perform well in the time remaining on your old job. Just as important, the agreement allows you to push back on further requests to help out on your old job once you are in your new position. You identified the work to do, you did it, and transitioned the rest and your manager agreed with the plan. That means it is your old manager's problem, not yours.

After meeting with your manager about the transition, you will need to set up tracking for the tasks to complete as well as the work that will transition to a new person. Without setting up a plan for this work, you won't really know if you can get the work done in the short time left before you start your new position.

Getting agreement with your manager about all of the work that you will do and what you will transition helps make the transition right for you and for your old team. Plus, getting the work done means you leave with your good reputation intact as you start your new position.

Goals for Your New Position

What do you define as success in your new dream job?

In the coming chapters, we're going to go through a comprehensive list of what you need to do in your new position so that you are successful. Success, however, means different things to different people. One person may consider a new position successful if they break into a new career in a new industry while keeping the paycheck whole from their old career and industry. Someone else may consider a new position successful if they are able to get along with their manager and the rest of their team. Or someone else may consider success as simply working less than 60-hour weeks, so that they get to spend time with the family.

What we need to do, then, before we start our new job, is to define goals as to what we would consider success in the new job. Without these goals to take what we learn in our first 30 days, we will have no ability to measure our success taking this new position. Not whether we are successful in completing tasks for our manager and team, but whether or not we get what we want from the position. The world is filled with people who complete task after task, project after project, yet are unhappy in their work. By defining success goals for our new position, we have the ability to evaluate the position and objectively determine how close we are to what we wanted from the job.

So what kinds of goals should we set?

The first type of goal to set is about the types of job skills that we want to acquire from the position. Over the long haul, careers are built on continuously adding to our job skills—programming new languages, increasing the size of our projects we manage, or doubling the size of our budget responsibilities, for example.

Thus, part of our goals for our dream job should be to define what job skills we will improve as the result of taking this job. Is it increased responsibilities? Is learning about a skill adjacent to our current skill the primary goal? Or is learning about an area of work we've missed in the past part of the appeal of our new job?

The second type of goal to set is the personal goals for the job. These are goals that are not necessarily interesting to your next potential employer, but are important to your work satisfaction. For some people, working on a job that gives them enough time with their family is a driving factor and, if this is a goal for you, you will need to ensure the new job provides this or you will not have happiness in your work.

For other people, a goal for the job is to do well so the position will lead to a promotion at work. This type of motivation then requires you to evaluate the new job based on ensuring it has what it takes to position you for the promotion in the time frame you want.

Other people could have a goal that the people they work with fit their values and lifestyles; that the culture of work matches the type of culture the person thrives in doing their work. Some people love a culture of conflict while others want collaboration. If you thought your view of the culture was one way and starting on the job you discover it is different, it will result in unhappiness in doing your work.

Not that there should only be one type of personal goal with a position; several make sense. If your ideal working environment is one where you learn about stuff on the job you didn't know, where people collaborate in the work and managers have a hands-off approach in letting you do your work, then those goals need to have reality checked against them when you start the job.

Without clearly defining your goals for the new position, you will lose valuable time in deciding if the job is right for you. You will expend precious days determining what you can do to change what is happening at work that doesn't match up with some undefined perception in your head that is making you uncomfortable at work. Plus, the longer your inability to evaluate your job against what you want from the job, the more likely unhappiness will visit your work and poor work performance will occur.

By writing out your goals for the new position, you will get an additional benefit: you now have the ability to continuously evaluate your job based on your goals over time, not just the first 30 days on the job. If your dream job matches your goals and a year later a new manager starts running the department and changes direction, you have a readymade list to check if the change is good for you or if it is time to start looking for a new job.

Or, the goals you originally had for the position were good, but the job offered much more than you originally saw and you made the goals for the work bigger.

Thus, your new position should give you improving job skills and meet your personal goals for work. By writing these goals down, you have the ability every day, every week, and every month to determine if the job is the right one for you. Without these goals, you will lose valuable time getting to the "is this job right for me right now?" answer you need to decide to stay in a position or to start looking for a new one.

How Long Will The Position Last?

And that brings us to the final factor you need to decide about your new position: how long will the job last?

It may seem ridiculous to think about leaving a job before you even start it, but your long-term career success depends on it. Every job ends. Every project ends. And, given a recession, every company has a good shot at ending through bankruptcy or buyouts.

This was brought home to me working early in my career. I was pulled from my current job to work on a big, five-state project. I went from 40-hour workweeks to 60-hour workweeks and maintained that pace for almost 18 months. I won awards for the work, shout-outs from managers about how good the project went and I objectively knew I had done a good job. Two weeks before the end of the job, my manager told me that there was no position for me when the project ended; I needed to go interview for open positions or I was most likely going to be laid off. I had missed this important lesson that all jobs end and you need to find your next gig.

People working as consultants understand that jobs end. When consultants go on assignment, they work as part of the contract between their consulting firm and the company where they are doing the consulting assignment. The contracts have end dates and a significant amount of time is spent determining if the contract will really end or will extend for some period of time.

Consultants know that at the end of the current contract, they need to have already found another contract to work or they are put on what is called the "bench." If the consultant doesn't land another contract after being on the bench, the consultant is let go.

Consequently, consultants are very tuned into understanding how long a job will last. As soon as they see something change in their opinion of how long a position lasts, they immediately do something about it. They tap their networks to look for work. They call other contractors to find suitable openings. They don't wait for bad news; they go after the next position based on when they think the current position will end.

Full-time employees rarely think about when the job will end. Yet, if you thought the job would last for two years, you'd start looking for another job a year in advance. Or, if you thought you'd attain your job goals in a year and were on track for doing that in nine months, you'd start looking for your next position. Or, if the circumstances of your job changed, say with a buyout from another company, you'd immediately re-evaluate how long the position would last.

When you think through how long a position will last, just like establishing job skill and personal goals for the job, you have a baseline measurement for your work to compare to when reality hits you on the Monday morning you start your next job. You can revise what you think about the job over time, of course—even changing your goals. But not having the goals and how long you think the job will last before you start will leave you drifting in the workplace. Drifting in the workplace is not the sign of a successful professional.

Alright. You've tied up all the loose ends at your old position. You've got your job skills and personal goals for the job figured out. And you have a good idea for how long the job will last before it is time to start looking anew.

You are ready for Monday—your first day on the new job.

Chapter

3 | Week One

Access to Corporate Resources

The first day on a new job—especially your dream job—is exciting in that you are experiencing something new, anxious because you have cast away the old and replaced it with something unknown, and tedious because of the administrative paperwork that goes along with starting a new job. Then, later on, you will likely feel overwhelmed from all the information overload you are getting learning about your dream job, manager, team, and company. Since all of it is new, you pay equal attention to everything. Paying attention to everything, of course, is tiring and overwhelming at the same time. Until you can figure out what is important and how to prioritize your work, you will continue to have anxious moments and wonder if you are doing the right stuff at the right time or giving it the right degree of importance.

All of this is normal. Instead of worrying about all of these different feelings, simply go with the flow knowing that they will sort themselves out as you move forward. Plus, what we're working on here is giving you a way to gauge your progress week-by-week so that you can determine if you are understanding the work and what needs doing.

Each week of the first four weeks on your dream job will have specific goals for you to accomplish. The reason for weekly goals is that specific tasks to do day-by-day are too often trumped by events that happen that are out of your control. "Oh, you started just in time to come to our three-day offsite planning event," your manager will say. Tough to meet with customers then, isn't it?

So, instead, there are goals for each week. The goals are designed to start with personal stuff you can control and then build on that to work with your team, then your stakeholders, and then your customers. For example, it makes sense to have as much information about your dream job as possible before going out and speaking with your customers of your work. And if you are invited to a weeklong event with your customers your first week on your dream job, you can grab those goals and know what needs doing with them.

When I think of week one, I think of *access*, *meeting and greeting*, *organization*, and *work goals*. Each is critical to getting to success after 30 days in your dream job, and, while mundane, are needed to complete tasks that your manager is giving you.

Access

Access is getting the right permissions to use the resources of the company. You need access to systems, company benefits, building entrances, e-mail accounts, databases or whatever you need to help the company in your role.

It starts, when working with a new company in the United States, with the filling out of an I-9 form where you document your permission to work in the country. If you are a United States citizen, you need a passport or two official government forms of identification. If you are not a United States citizen, then you need to bring the documentation that shows you can work in this country.

This is mundane, but important. Companies need to have this information within your first few days of work, so getting this done the first day and out of the way clears the deck for the rest of the access issues you need. Bring your documentation to work with you on your first day.

After that, usually someone will help you sign up for the various benefits the company provides their employees. The help could be in the form of paper signups for benefits or a link to a URL on a website where you, as a new employee, can sign up for the company benefits. Our purpose here is not to tell you what benefits to sign up for, but instead, to ensure that you get this done and off your checklist of things to do starting with a company.

Most of the time, this type of access and benefits are not much of an issue—just make sure they get done.

On the other hand, the rest of the access to company resources can really help or hurt your ability to get results on your new job.

People, working in today's information society, need access to company computers, software programs, and a workspace. How well companies provide these resources is all over the map and gives you your first clue as to how well your new company or department within a company will match up to your job needs.

For example, in one Fortune 100 company I worked for, it took three weeks to get a laptop. It was my first indication that the way this company managed their business was not the best. I ended up taking my personal laptop to work and accessing my e-mail through the Internet e-mail portal for the company.

At another Fortune 100 company, for example, acquiring your computer and access to systems is entirely up to you. Have setup issues? You need to solve them yourself. Need help from a technical department? Here's the phone number—go ahead and call them.

Of course, not all companies are like this. If you walked into the first day of your new job and your manager took you to your cubicle, equipped with laptop, a second monitor, a list of all the software programs you need with how to access them and introduced you to your teammate charged with helping you get up-to-speed on the software programs, would you be impressed? I would. Plus, you would immediately understand that for getting people on board to start working, this company or manager knows how to get it done.

Would that affect your view of working for the company? Would you want to work for the company that took three weeks to get you a laptop, or work for the company where you walked in the door and your access was all done?

Most companies are somewhere between these extremes. Your challenge, then, is to ensure that you have a checklist of programs you need access to and track them until your access is completed.

This is not as easy as it sounds. Most people do not know the interactions and access to programs that they use on their jobs. This is not an indictment of their capabilities, but rather, a reflection that most people's jobs are to do something in the business and all their tools are done through a technology department. How the technology is set up is not part of their job.

But access is access, so the new person in a job is often left thinking they have everything they need, but, in reality, don't have all the tools for the work.

Here's your quick list of access needed for your work:

- **Access to the building**. Usually key cards. This includes the doors plus any stairwells between floors if you are in a multi-story office building. Ask if you have access 24-hours a day and on weekends—not that you'll be using it all weekend, but coming in to work on a Saturday and not having your key card work is a disheartening experience.

- **Access to your cubicle**. This includes getting to your cubicles as well as keys to open and lock your desk drawers. Have access to a common set of file cabinets? Need to locate them so you know where they are to use.

- **Your benefits**. One of the big reasons for working is access to benefits. Health insurance, disability insurance, life insurance...gym memberships. You need to know both how to sign up for the benefits, and also how to check balances (like in your 401(k) account) and maintain the benefits. Sometimes, benefits are not available until later in your employment, so those should get noted on your calendar so when the time comes you have a reminder.

- **Your work computer**. This is mostly ensuring that you have one, but one needs to check that the client software programs, like the client your company uses for e-mail, is already installed on the computer.

- **Your software systems**. Many, if not most, company work is done on software programs accessed through the company intranet. Some companies are also accessing corporate systems that are in the "computing cloud" that require Internet access as well. All of these user names, passwords, and access levels need to be verified for your work.

So start making a list—or ask for one—of all the programs you need access to for your work. E-mail access done? Check. Company intranet? Check. Access to the company's systems while working from home? Still waiting. Blackberry—or iPhone? Still waiting.

Making a list and keeping track of it sounds simple. It is. But most people keep the list in their heads and then get to crunch time three-and-a-half weeks after starting the job. Then they go to their manager and say they can't complete the work because they don't have access to the right systems. And their manager wonders where they were for the last three weeks because they never mentioned it as a problem.

The deal with access is this: it provides you a way to evaluate the company and management team in their ability to give you the tools you need to do your job. Plus, it gives you the ability to produce results faster when access is taken care of up front, helping you fit into the team. Without quickly getting access to systems, you can't get to ac-complishment.

The Dance of Meet and Greet

Meeting and greeting often happens in the first day or two on the job. You and your manager or a trusted teammate get to walk around the floor or building and meet people you work with. If it is a small company, you might meet everyone. If it's a large company, you might just meet people in the department.

Meeting and greeting is just that: meeting and greeting. Usually, no substantive conversation occurs, but you at least get to put a name with a face—and hopefully, you remember the name. Consider it like being at a party where, perhaps, you know no one and the host walks around with you and introduces you to every person there.

When meeting and greeting people, I'd suggest following some basic principles:

- **Keep the meet and greet short**—you are interrupting people who are in the middle of doing their work. People usually don't want to spend 15 minutes with you; they would rather spend two minutes or less so they can continue working.

- **Ask questions and talk less**—the important part here is that you really don't know the team culture. The questions you should ask are questions that will help you remember this person's name, their role, or their impact on your work.

- **Have three or four stock responses to meeting a person**. If you meet twenty people, your manager will wonder about your social capabilities if all you ever respond to meeting someone is "It was a pleasure to meet you." You need to vary it a bit—"I'm looking forward to working with you," "It is great to work with you," "I'm very happy to meet you"—all can help give you a variety of responses in meeting people.

- **Meet managers the same way you meet your team**. If you treat meeting your manager's manager differently than you treat meeting your teammates, your manager will wonder if all you do is "manage up" well and throw your teammates under a bus. People are people and meeting them the same, professional way will not raise any red flags. Remember, you're evaluated the minute you start in a new job.

- **Do not use humor in meeting and greeting**. Humor style varies from person to person. My irony doesn't match up with falling down physical humor and that doesn't match up with satire. In a short meeting and greeting situation, throwing out one-liners is almost guaranteed to fail. Humor can come later.

- **Ask people you know the context for your work now in your dream job**. Perhaps you are simply moving to a different team in the same company and you know many of the people you will work with. That's great—but don't assume what they do in your new job is the same relationship they had with you in your old job. Your role has changed (is the change easier for them, or is it now threatening them?) and perhaps their role interfacing with you has changed as well. The key is to ensure that you ask their relationship to your new role and make no assumptions about the relationship.

The other issue on meeting and greeting is that many people will not be at their desk in their cubes when you come by to meet them. You and your manager end up staring at the inside of a cubicle while your manager explains that Mary is a key person to know for your work and she isn't there. Just her yellow duck sitting there on top of her desk.

Cubicles create a mouse maze, but try and remember the person's location by something unique in the cubicle—the yellow duck sitting on top of the desk—so that you can find it again. When you are done meeting and greeting and your manager departs for other tasks, take some of your free time and swing by the cubicles of the people you missed and see if they are there.

Greeting people in this manner follows the same rules as meeting them with your manager. It is just good social practice to make the attempt to meet someone one-on-one before you show up in your first team meeting and half the people there assume that you are the new person, but don't know for sure.

Meeting and greeting people on your new team is usually a simple affair—as long as you don't make any social mistakes that can start you off on the wrong foot with your team. Following these guidelines will help make that first contact with your new team great.

The Organization

Business is a social enterprise—we get things done by working with people. Plus we receive other people's work and send our work on to others. To help understand where we get work and where we send our work, companies create organizations to help clarify roles and responsibilities. We then see how the organization is defined through organization charts.

Unfortunately, most managers don't provide a clear picture of either the organization or how the organization is supposed to work. What happens instead is a verbal description of what you do and who you get your work from.

Yet, understanding how the business is supposed to work through your team is critical to your contributing to your team's success. The best way to get up to speed quickly is to ask your manager to explain the current organization chart to you. Doing so will give you the manager's perspective on how it is all supposed to work. Plus, between the explanation and your questions, it will start to give you the context of the thinking behind the way the business is set up.

The Big Picture

Different people think differently. Some think from big picture down to details and others think from details up to big picture. Whichever way you think, start the explanation of the organization chart there. Regardless of where you start, by the end of the explanation you will want lots of details about your team and department interactions.

Make sure you get explanations of each of the headings of the organization chart for at least your division or, if the company is smaller, of the entire company. What you want to learn is the relationships between the divisions or departments and how all of that is supposed to work.

For example, is information technology set up as an independent department? How do the needs of the business get to information technology so work can get done? Or, how does customer service interact with sales?

Once you see the big boxes, you will quickly see the thought process behind the management of the company. Is the organization set up as a functional organization? Like Sales, Finance, and Information Technology, regardless of the customer? Or is it set up around customer groups with the functional areas embedded in the customer group? Or is it set up around product lines? Or is it some hybrid?

Different ways of organizing companies have implications in how you get your work done. If everything is self-contained in your division, that could make your work easier if all you do is stay in your division—and harder if you have to step outside of it.

Understanding the approach a company uses also gives you insight later when organizations change, something they always do. If the organization was distributed and now goes centralized, it is easier to understand the change by knowing how the organization is set up now. If the organization was functional and now switches to a product orientation, it gives you context that you can use to adjust to the changes.

The other important characteristic of organizations is that even though the organization is titled "information technology" it is rarely called "information technology." Instead, the organization is called by the name of the leader heading up the organization. "We need to talk to someone in John Smith's group to get that done." Like we know who "John Smith" is when we start out at a new company.

Without knowing the names of the people leading the different departments, especially the ones you will interact with in your work, it will take you longer to understand the relationships between departments and feel comfortable interacting with people in your new role.

If your new job is part of the same company, you will know the names of the people leading the organizations. In that case, there is a good possibility that how you interact with the different groups will change in your new role. If you know all the names of the people running the organizations, concentrate on understanding the way the interactions are handled with the people in the organization, looking for differences from your previous roles in the company.

The intent of understanding the big picture of an organization is to start building context and background faster for your job. If it takes you three months to learn who "John Smith's" organization is and how they can help you, you will miss out on opportunities to do your job better or feel comfortable discussing your work with others. People who understand how the business is set up do better reacting to changes in the business.

The Small Picture

Where the explanations of the departments and their roles can easily be explained with a minimum of detail, you will need to change that level when it gets to the people giving you work to do, your team, and where the output of your work goes. Here, you want lots of details to understand the work.

The small picture is really two parts. First, there is the organization chart that gives you roles and responsibilities of the people in the roles. Then, second, there is the actual workflow that goes on so that work gets done. Ideally, the organizational chart would be the same as the workflow diagram because it makes sense to lay out the organization the same way the work is done. Rarely is that the case, however.

Once you are past the big picture of the organization chart, you now want to break down your department and team into much smaller details. Your purpose here is to understand the roles in your team and the roles of the people where you get your work and where you send the output of your work.

"Role" means what that person does on the team. You can have ten people who perform the same function—handle escalated support tickets, for example—each of whom handles different types of escalated tickets. "Joe" handles escalated tickets relating to computer issues whereas "Mary" handles tickets relating to Microsoft Windows software. It's the same "role" in terms of the fact that each handles escalated support tickets, but each person has a specialty within the role.

By doing this with each person on the team—remember, this is the manager telling you the role—you will get how the manager is viewing what people are doing to achieve the department goals. This is useful when, next week, we look at how each individual views their role on the team.

Understanding the role of each person on the team is important for you in your work. Each role tells you where to get help with the specifics of your work. Additionally, these roles will help you determine how your unique job skills and background can make the team better than it is now. If all you do on a team is the same as three others on the team that is not as valuable as doing the same thing as three others on the team *plus deploying a unique skill that helps achieve business objectives*.

Now, you may have been hired to perform that unique job skill and already know what it is. But most of the time, you are hired to perform a specific function and your unique contributions to the team come about later. Working to understand each person's role on a team from a manager's viewpoint gives you a baseline to evaluate how you can contribute more to the team than just what your job description states.

The key here is to understand the role of each person who provides input to your work, who can help you get the work done, and who your work goes to after your part is done (your customer, whether internal or external).

The second portion of the small picture is understanding the workflow as it relates to the organization. Every position on the team has a workflow, documented or not. This workflow is how you are expected to do the work, who you are expected to work with, and who your work goes to when your part is done.

Now, your manager may not know the workflow for your job past "this group does this, gives it to us, we do this with it, and give it to that group when we're done." That's okay as far as it goes. What you really want to have, though, is the workflow diagram and *the name of each person responsible for each part of the diagram*. It is great to understand the theory, but business is a social medium and we get work done through people.

Knowing the names of these people gives us the ability—which we will use later—to go and interview them so that we can understand their view on how work gets done and comes to us or how our work affects the person we give our work to when we're done with our part.

In concluding this kind of meeting, where there is tons of information provided and all of it is brand new to you, you will most likely feel over-whelmed. Certainly you will feel information overload. You won't remember all of it, so you need to take good notes during the session.

Doing this, however, gets you up to speed faster. First, you hear your manager's viewpoint on the organization. This is critical, as you need to "fit" in with the manager and the team.

Second, you will have heard the whole story once and that gets you on the road faster than hearing about the organization piecemeal over time. You want the manager to fit the pieces of the puzzle together for you, not to have you single-handedly figuring out each piece and making up how it fits together.

Third, you will want to consolidate your notes. Whenever I consolidate notes from meetings, I am forced to organize them in a way that con-tributes to my learning. Consolidating notes means you can explain the notes to another person, which helps you learn faster.

Finally, consolidating your notes will tell you where you were unclear about something and gives you the ability to go back to your manager to clarify what you wrote and how it fits, giving you a more complete picture of the organization.

The faster you can get to know the organization and the roles of the people in it, the faster you will get to producing results for your manager and team.

The Importance of Administrivia

There are also details for communication within the manager's realm of work. Every manager has standard methods of communication. This standard method is all about the underlying way a team communicates and runs itself. For example, status reports vary in format and type of information from manager to manager. So does a way to get notified about absences and vacations and recurring meetings with the team. All of this administration stuff may seem trivial, yet this "administrivia" is how the department runs with no effort from the manager. The more stuff that happens automatically, without requiring managerial intervention, the better able the team is to focus on better results doing harder tasks.

While every manager has a different way of getting this information, within each manager is a preferred method of communication.

Something as simple as a status report can have wide ranges of needed information for that manager. For example, one manager will want a consistent set of numbers to report in the status that happen to match up with the goals for the department. Another will want to know what has been completed during the week, regardless of the activities done for the week to get to the results. It isn't the meeting that is important, but the result of your work after the meeting is done.

Some managers will have weekly team meetings, others will do them quarterly and still others will only have them when they are needed.

The easy task is to get plugged into the communication process of your manager and schedule the meetings in your calendar.

Many people underestimate the importance of this seemingly trivial communication stuff. Status reports, for example, are routinely ignored or mismanaged. Yet, this consistent communication is a perfect way for you to show your work to your manager. Or show how poor you are at doing good work. Every week you have the opportunity to show results or show work that doesn't lead to results.

You may have previously reported to a manager who only valued accomplishments in the status report. Twenty meetings that week? Who cares? If it took you twenty meetings to get to a decision on a project, then the result is the action on the product, not the meetings.

Your current manager may want the result, but also want listed all twenty meetings from the week on the status report. The manager may want to be invited to every meeting even though the manager doesn't attend, just to see what people are doing. All of these, by the way, are real examples.

If you don't ask about these communications methods, you will discover them as you go along—by not doing them right. Your manager will ask if you've attended any meetings and then ask why they are not on the status report. Or your manager will ask why you are going to so many meetings and not getting anything done! Managers know how this is done with their team and you are now on the team and, of course, the manager easily assumes you know how to do a status report and do team meetings. It is an assumption you cannot make.

The only way to win is to start getting the communication correct right away—and quickly fit into the manager's management style—by asking. What goes in the status report? What is the format for it? Do you have team meetings? Are the team members expected to bring standard stuff to each team meeting that you should prepare? When are the team meetings? Are they face-to-face when everyone is in the same building, or can you attend via a conference call? How do you get the meeting invitations for both team meetings and other recurring departmental meetings?

These communication practices are rarely laid out for a new person to see. Yet, the manager and the current team practice the communication methods every day. By asking and integrating yourself into these communication practices and then asking for feedback when you first start using them, you will make giant leaps towards quickly "fitting in" with the team.

While one objective is fitting in with the team, you can also learn a great deal from these communication methods about your new manager and team.

The lowly status report, for example, is a great way to find out what is important to the manager. Seriously, if all the manager is looking to see on a status report is the meetings you attended (and I had one like this), then it is easy to conclude that activities are more important than results.

It also is a way to differentiate your work from that of your co-workers. If all that is required is the meetings you attended during the week, then most will simply list those meetings. If you list the meetings *and* the results from your performance for the week, then you can show superior results every week.

A good list for administrivia is this one:

- **Status Reports**. You will need to know if they are done, when they are due, what content needs to be in them, what format you should use, and the level of detail needed. Is there a common format?

- **Team Meetings**. You need to be on the invite list for the meetings, know the format, know if you need to prepare something for each one, and the purpose of the meetings.

- **Vacation Requests**. You need to know how to make vacation requests, how far in advance to make them from when you have your vacation, and what departmental rules there are for taking them (only one person out during a specific holiday, for example).

- **Reporting a sick day**. When you are sick, who do you call? Do you also send an e-mail out to your team—if you have access to company e-mail from home? What is the proper process to follow?

- **Recurring management meetings**. Often there are quarterly skip-level management meetings held to bring the entire group together to get on the same page. You need to be added to the invitation list, especially since someone outside your new department usually keeps the list.

Once you know the favored communication methods, you now have the ability to evaluate how successfully the methods are working. Do people follow the methods? Complain about them? Does the manager follow through with them?

The key here is to proactively get locked into the standard communication and meeting practices of your new manager. Ask, rather than be wrong and get corrected by your manager or team member. You'll fit in faster, and you won't make obvious errors undermining your success early on the job.

Get Your Goals On

Businesses have objectives that need accomplishing, whether it is a sales number, an expense reduction number or a cycle time that needs reducing. These overall business objectives then trickle down to divisions, departments, managers—and you. You can tell a lot about your manager from the goals that are set for you and the team.

In addition, goals are most often used in your performance review as the largest chunk of what you accomplished from your work. This makes sense; the most important work you do on the job is accomplishing the goals of the business that are translated for you by your goals given to you by your manager.

The goals you get also provide a convenient constraint on what work you do. If your manager, for example, is assigning you work that isn't part of your goals, it is perfectly legitimate to ask why the work is more important than your current goals. Or if you should revisit your goals to include the work asked for—and eliminate something that is no longer needed. Thus, your goals become the framework, the boundaries, of what you work on in the job.

During your first week, then, you should get a set of goals for you to start working on.

It is not the intent of this book to provide all the information on how to set up effective goals. There is plenty of good information on that subject out there already. What you do want to do, however, is ensure that you have *your department goals* and *your personal goals*.

When you were listening to the organization chart information from your manager, you were getting the roles and responsibilities of each of the different groups of people in the organization. Well, those roles and responsibilities translate into goals for each of the different groups. Since your manager should be evaluated on the performance of the team being managed, the department goals give you a clear picture of what needs getting done by the overall team led by your manager.

Going over the department goals also gives you a sense of the priority of work in the department. Is all the concentration of work in the department on one goal? That tells you the importance of making that goal.

Or is it on two specific goals? Asking about the goal to seek understanding will help you know what is important in the department. Asking
about the priority of the goal to the work right now will give you an indication of what work needs doing right now compared to later.

At the other end of the scale, some managers will pull out their goals,
you will ask about the most important work going on in the department,
and your manager will answer back with something totally not on the
goals shown to you. That's a red flag because departments need to
work on achieving their goals—or the goals need to change.

Once you understand the department goals, an organized manager will
have your individual goals ready for you.

While we won't cover how to set up effective goals, there are some goal
characteristics that will tell you a lot about your new position and the
effectiveness of the team.

Goals tell attainment stories

If you have a goal to lose ten pounds, it isn't just a goal. Instead, it is a
goal with a story of how you will achieve losing the ten pounds.

The same is true in your department. If you have a goal to reduce cycle
time for a particular process by three days, there should be a story
about how the department is working to achieve that goal. Do you
reduce cycle time by adding more inventory so orders go out faster? Or
are we installing a new conveyor line to move the product more quickly
to the front? Or are you rearranging the inventory so the fastest moving
items are in the front?

There are hundreds of methods of affecting cycle time in a process.
The key is in understanding how the group will go about it with this particular process. There should be a "we're going to achieve this goal
by..." statement. Not that the work associated with the statement is
easy, but that the goal has a story for attaining it.

If the answer to "how are you planning on achieving this goal?" is a be-
wildered look, then you are either the answer—our hero—or you
should plan on big issues with achieving the goal.

You need control to achieve goals

When you are listening to your department or personal goals, a key ingredient in getting to success is having control over the outcome of the goal.

When you are listening to the story of how to attain the goal, you should ask if the department (or you, for your goals) is dependent on others to achieve the goal. If the answer is that making the goal is dependent on two other departments who don't share a common manager or are dependent on approvals from five different committees, the goal will be that much more difficult to achieve.

Most department goals are dependent on other departments or functions in the company to make the goal. The degree of difficulty for achieving the goal goes up higher the more people that are involved.

For your personal goals, the same is true. If you are dependent on five other people on your team to supply you with stuff on time over the course of three months, your goal is more difficult to achieve than if you were doing the entirety of the work yourself.

The same principle for department goals applies here as well: the more dependent you are on other people to achieve your goal, the more difficult the goal will be to achieve.

Goals need to measure your performance, not the team or department performance

Most companies can measure performance to a particular department, though not necessarily a particular manager. Few companies do a good job of measuring individual performance on specific goals. Most corporate reporting systems are designed to measure to a department level (with the exception of Sales, where they need to pay commissions).

Changing the reporting systems to measure individual performance is often expensive and time consuming with the only benefit of enabling you to judge your attainment to your goals. Yet, companies will speak to the importance of the SMART Goal measurement, but when you dig inside the goal, it is not measurable to the level of your work.

Measuring your progress to your goals is critical for giving you early warning of problems in achieving your goals. You want measurement systems for your individual performance so you can differentiate your work from others for your performance review. You want measurement systems that allow you to know if you are successful independent of your manager's subjective opinion. Without this independent ability to measure your success or failure, you won't be as fully engaged in the work as you could or should be.

Think, for example, about "team" goals. Most teams have them because team goals help cement and orient the team towards a common cause. That's good. But when it comes to assigning performance review ratings to your performance, team goals drag the average rating down because the goal measures the team, not you. If you can't measure the performance of an individual's contribution to a team goal, high performing team members will have their performance rating dragged down by the average or poor performing team members on team goals. That lowers your overall rating as well—and costs you money when pay raises and bonuses are doled out based on performance review ratings.

When you are listening to your goals for the department or for your work, ask hard questions about how the progress for the goals is measured. Ask how the measurement shows an individual's performance, especially for team goals.

In the end, the less the ability to measure your individual work, the more your performance review will be based on your manager's perceptions of your work. Plus, your manager, in defending the rating, will have fewer facts about your performance to justify the rating compared to solid performance measurements.

As a new person, you won't be able to change the department goals or yours on the first day on the job. The intent here is to both understand your goals so you can start working them and to provide you with a window into your new performance environment. If none of the goals are measurable, for example, it tells you the management team will evaluate you on their perception of your work which, in turn, will drive your behavior about how you report your completed work. Or, there could be great measurements in place to determine your contribution and that tells you that the management team has thought through how great performing teams do their work.

No environment is perfect when it comes to goals. High performing individuals want their performance measured because they thrive on achieving their goals. Having mushy ratings systems where performance is just perception will put each person in jeopardy for getting the performance rating they deserve.

The reasons to get your goals early after starting the job is that they give you the foundation for understanding the priorities of your work, a focus for asking questions about the work, and help you in determining how appropriate the goals are three weeks from now when you get to the end of your first 30 days on your new dream job.

Weekly Review—Week One

It was a long and tiring week in your new job, wasn't it? Well, even though you got to Friday, your week isn't done just yet.

What happens in new positions is that the new person gets information overload. With the information overload comes anxiety, joy, thrill, despair, and dozens of other emotions depending on everything about your dream job. Plus, there is uncertainty. Will the dream job work out? Will my team like me? My manager seems like he is okay, but there's just something about him that makes me wonder...what?

It is easy to simply take in that first week and hit the weekend and relax. You've gone with the flow and now it is time for the flow to stop.

Not really. I'd suggest taking one more step at the end of each of your weeks on your new dream job. That step is a weekly review.

Now, David Allen in his ground-breaking productivity book *Getting Things Done* advocates taking a weekly review of all of your outstanding tasks so that you gain control through the perspective of reviewing what you have done.

So it is here with your objectives for the new job. Now is the time to get perspective, review your activities for the week, and determine what still needs accomplishing during the next week. Each week, get out all of your notes, a separate piece of paper or blank screen on your computer, and get ready for a review.

There are big benefits to doing the review.

First, you will stay relatively organized. I say relatively because whenever you are in a new position, how you organized yourself before might not be exactly the same for the new job. You may still be tweaking what you think works, what you thought was important, or your expectations about the dream job versus the reality of how it is working during the week.

This weekly review ensures that the big objectives for the week—access, organization and goals—are reviewed and organized as done or not. The review helps determine if what you did before you started on your first day is really done as well. Staying organized in these areas ensures that nothing falls through the cracks and gives you much-needed perspective about the new job.

Second, the review tamps down the wild swings in emotions about the new job. Up, down, it all happened during the week. By going through your objectives for the week and deciding if you met them you will get focus on what worked and what needs work.

This focus takes the emotional swings away so that you can focus on your facts about the job. When you get your accomplishments down for the week, you "objectify" them by getting them out of your head. You may still have a ton of work to do and you may still not feel good about how you are adapting to the position, but at least you will separate what is working and what isn't in the review. Or you may have accomplished your objectives for the week and are euphoric over the job; your review will give you additional areas where you can focus and find out even more.

Third, the review gives you lists of what should have happened but didn't. This creates your follow-up list for your manager, team, and support in the company. Didn't get access to a particular system during the week you should have had? Down it goes on the list. Supposed to have gotten info on your 401(k) contributions from Human Resources but didn't? Down it goes on the list.

This follow-up list is important for you in that progress is made on getting acclimated into the position. Plus, coming back and asking for what is promised from your manager, team, and support team in the company sends a strong signal that you get it, expect what was promised, and will follow through on getting results. This immediately establishes a personal brand of organization, results orientation, and follow-up.

Fourth, the weekly review identifies areas that you understand, still do not understand or need clarifying. When you got the department goals and are now reviewing the notes, you now don't see how one particular goal was going to be achieved. Or you see that a goal you have is measured by a system you don't have access to and wasn't on your list.

By identifying areas that need clarification, you solidify what you think you know now and what you think you don't know. The truth is somewhere in between, of course, but getting solid knowledge identified and understood—that what you are sure about in the job—helps give you confidence about the position. The more "solid knowledge" you have about the job, the less you have to focus on it; it is just known and you can move on to the next level.

It's just like electricity; most of the time we don't have to worry about lights coming on when we flip a switch and we move on to other things. But if we constantly have to worry about the lights coming on when we flip the switch, it is much tougher to make progress. If we have to worry about everything on the job, we'll never make progress on the job.

Finally, the weekly review will give you another level of learning. Doing the review means going through the objectives for the week and seeing if you made them. You will discover what is meeting your expectations about the job, manager, and team and what isn't. You'll see if what carries over into the second week is still there the third week.

Reviewing these weekly objectives will let you look at the notes from the meeting on Tuesday on goals and settle whether or not you understand the goals. In essence, you will see the information three times—once when you got the information from your manager, again when you consolidated your notes after the meeting, and now during the weekly review when you once more reinforce what you learned.

This may seem a bit of overkill—seriously; three times you go through notes? But remember our objective here is to get up to speed as quickly as possible in the first thirty days to both show some results in the job as well as make a good assessment if the position is meeting your personal objectives for the job.

I would plan on spending up to six hours reviewing this information for the first week and up to four hours in the subsequent three weeks. The reason the first week takes so long is that you need to review the objectives from before starting the job as well as the information overload from week one. There is more information overload in the first week of a new job, especially in a new company, than during other weeks. Information in subsequent weeks is focused on getting your job done after getting a baseline about the company, department, goals, and benefits. It is still a lot of information, but the information is more about your job skills.

Your first weekly review should consider the following:

- **Access**. Here you review your long list of acquiring access to company resources—the building, your cubicle, benefits, systems, and your computer. All nailed down? Or are you still missing critical access to systems that help you do your job that need follow-up next week?

- **Meet and Greet**. If all you were able to do in the first week is to quickly meet your new teammates, now is the time to write down your first impressions of them. Not that this impression is written in stone, but it helps you recognize people and is a first step in having a comparison to check against as you get to know the person better. Plus, did you miss meeting anyone on the team? Were they on vacation or out of town on business for the week? In this case, mark on your calendar or task management system to meet the person early in the next week.

- **Organization – departments**. A good practice is to take each area of the organization and write down the role the organization plays either in the company or as it relates to your department. Sure, finance is finance, but what area of finance is the one you need to learn about in your new job? Or, if you are in finance, who do you support and what is their role in the organization? If you can't easily explain the roles within the company, now is the time to write your questions down so when you meet with your manager the next time, you can ask follow-up questions to help clarify your thinking.

- **Organization – your team**. For each member of your team, you should be able to write down their role on the team as viewed by your manager and the way the person will interact with you in your work. It might be that all of you on your team do the same functional thing "we handle escalated support tickets for X," or "we provide critical care nursing in ICU," but usually each person on the team has unique critical skills. Sure, you may know the XYZ program better than anyone else on your team, but Joe knows the ABC program better than anyone else. That's what you want to capture—what is each person's specialty on the team according to your manager? Again, if you have a hard time writing this down, you'll need to get clarification from either your manager or your teammate in the next week.

- **Administrivia**. Administrivia, you will recall, is the underlying communication methods on the team, the recurring reports, methods of communicating and ongoing meetings the team uses in their work. If your manager does status reports, perhaps you've now done one in your first week. How did it go? Did it capture the right level of detail? Was it sent to the right place? Or you've had your first team meeting—how did that work out? The key here is that first, you need to have all this communication criteria down and on the calendar, and, second, you need to compare how the theory worked to the reality of it.

- **Goals**. Goals, in most organizations, become the foundation of the performance review. This first week is critical to getting the understanding of your goals. If you think you understand your goals, then the next three weeks on the job gives you the ability to evaluate how attainable the goal is for you. Or if you need to talk with your manager about the goal once the work is done. Go through each of your goals; note how you will attain the goal and how you will measure your progress. If you can't do either, or are unclear how to do either, it needs to get on your calendar to chat with your manager about the goals.

- **Our objective: Establish a corporate culture baseline.** Overall, what we are trying to do here in this first week is to establish a baseline of the culture—the rules, organization, underlying communications methods, and roles of the team. It is a baseline for understanding how the team and your manager do work. The baseline is important because the baseline is *what you are told*, not necessarily *how it is done in practice*. A *Cubicle Warrior* listens to what is said, but observes what is done, and comes to conclusions about what is observed. Remember, one of our primary goals in our dream job is to ensure it really is our dream job early on after starting. We do this by establishing baseline understandings of what is said and then compare it to what is done in practice.

- **Finally, how is the job compared to your personal objectives for it**? We went through a great amount of work before taking the job to ensure we knew what type of work we wanted to do, what kind of corporate culture supported our best work and the managerial style that helps us thrive on the job. Now is the time to pull out those objectives, go through each one and compare and contrast it with what you are seeing now in your dream job. Is it measuring up? Is it close? It's early, of course. But you should see signs validating your choice.

I would suggest doing one more task for the week: take your weekly review results and share them with your spouse, best friend, or other significant person in your life. The reason for doing this is that by having to explain what you found out about the organization and running through your first impressions of the team will force you to organize your thoughts: you have to explain it to someone else, which is always a great way to learn.

In addition, the person you are reviewing this with will challenge you in a nice way. Questions you will not have thought about will get asked. Will you have the answers? Maybe yes, maybe no, but the questions will help your learning process or will end up on your follow-up list for the next week. Plus, in sharing what you have learned, you tell the other person that they are important in your life as well.

Week one of a new job is usually the biggest week for overwhelm in starting a new job, especially if you are starting your dream job in a new company. Everything is new, even if your job skills are proven and needed in every company. New people, new goals, new manager, new cubicle, new commute, new building, new places to eat lunch and get coffee. All the newness can put people on edge, tire them out, and makes them question their confidence.

Paring down the unknowns about the work—getting your job to a base-line—really helps you get productive faster. The weekly review reveals what you think you know versus what you know you don't know quickly. Yes, this review takes a lot of time; I know that. But the benefits of doing the weekly review are quite significant—and something that most of your teammates don't do. By reviewing your week, you can significantly improve your chances of success on your dream job.

4 Week Two

Getting to Know Your Team

In the first week, you most likely spent a lot of time with your manager. This amount of time gives you a good sense of what you can expect from your manager and what your manager expects from you in return.

But there is another group of people, equally important, who affect your work. Those people are your teammates, the happy group of people that report to your manager and share in the workload. Your team helps you be a star—or a falling star. Teams are tricky, with their own micro-culture and intra-team conflicts. So working with your team is a challenge to get to your best work and to support the team getting to their best work.

There are many different types of teams. Organizationally, teams can be set up to do all one function—all people who do accounts payable, for example. All the salespeople in a region is another good example.

A different type of organizational team is one that has all the functions in it for a particular process in the organization. In home loans, for example, fulfilling the loan—the process between applying for a loan and getting it to closing—is done by an underwriter, a vendor manager who gets appraisals and external reports, and a closer. Each of these people work on the loan, accepting it from the sale of the loan to getting it to the people at the closing. Instead of having twenty underwriters and "throwing their work over the wall" to the next group, each team member in this organizational structure is dependent on each other to move the loan along.

A third type of team is an ad hoc, or "matrix managed" team. This is a team that comes together to solve a particular problem or work on a particular project, but each person on the team retains their own manager in the hierarchical organization. A matrix-managed team has a leader, typically a project manager, and moves the team through the work to completion. Once the work is done, the matrix-managed team disburses back to their normal departments.

Each of these different types of teams requires different approaches to integrating with them. Just to be clear, since you are the new kid on the team, it is usually your responsibility to integrate into the team, not everyone else integrating to your working style. This is why knowing what type of team works out best for your working style is so important when you are interviewing for a position.

The same function team

Integrating with the functional team starts with showing you have the job skills to do the work. Since everyone on the team does the same thing, if you don't have the right job skills, you'll be viewed as someone not ready for prime time and holding the team back.

Usually, not everyone has all the job skills necessary when they start a job—part of working a new job is to learn new job skills! The key, then, is to quickly identify what job skills are needed to get the work done, have someone on the team help you learn those skills, and then learn the skills as quickly as possible.

The interesting and fun part of functional teams is that, even though everyone works on the same function and theoretically the work is the same, different people end up more specialized within the function. If everyone on the team supports some customer application—repairing a telephone system, for example—the base work will be the same for everyone, but some will be better at some parts of the program than others.

Using our telephone application, for example, one person might be much better at the "dispatch a technician" function of the program. Another person on the team might be much better at the "move, add, and change order" function of the program. Another may be better at the "diagnostic testing" portion of the program.

Or, if everyone on the team does accounts receivable, one person might know receivables from corporations, another from non-profits, and a third from consumers. People will gravitate to that which they enjoy and will learn more about those areas because they enjoy working on them.

For you, then, working your team, you will need to show that you have the job skills to do the work. Then, your key is to find out the specialties that each person has on the team so that you know who to go to for help on that particular portion of the work.

In addition, knowing what each person specializes in will help you determine where you can add value to the team. If everyone is working on some part of the function except documentation—and you like documentation—then this might be an area where you can add value to the team.

The different function team

Our second type of team is one where each person performs one function in a process. In this type of team, when only one or two people perform a function in the process, the team is really as strong as its weakest link. Not only do you need to have the job skills to do the work, but you need to coordinate effectively between the other people on the team.

In comparison to the same function team, your challenge here is to learn each of the different functions done by the team. In essence, you need to learn the entire process being followed on the team and learn what each person does as part of the process. The learning curve with this type of team is steeper than with a same function team.

Your value on this type of team is performing your function at a high level so that it moves the team forward. You don't want to be the weakest link on this type of team as it holds the entire team back.

These types of teams offer you a way to learn "adjacent" skills to your own. Because each person on the team performs one function in the process, you have an input coming from someone on your team and your customer is someone else on your team. Learning how each of them do their jobs and then performing their tasks, say to cover vacations, is a great way to expand your portfolio of job skills.

The matrix-managed team

The matrix team is similar to the different function team in that each person on the matrix-managed team is brought to the team to perform a specific function. Your key focus on this type of team is to perform your function at the highest level possible so as to move the team forward.

The difference between a matrix-managed team and a different function team is that a matrix team has multiple managers. There is really no organizational control of the team by a team leader in a matrix-managed group. The team is dependent on the cooperation of the managers of each of the people on the team to get the work of the team done. In addition, the matrix team typically represents more than one "process" being performed as in a different function team.

The challenges of integrating into this type of team are to get your work done, have your manager support your work on the team, and quickly identify roadblocks on the team to the team leader and your manager. Matrix teams require more time to get to a decision because there are more managers who need to support the decision.

It is not like you can walk into your manager's office, get an answer and move forward. You need to work with the team leader, get an answer, and then have the team leader work with the impacted managers for approval.

Matrix teams give you a great opportunity to learn about other job skills. Because each person performs a different function and teams often have multiple business processes represented on the team, you are exposed to different job skills compared to other teams. Exposure to these skills is a valuable way to learn about other parts of the business and increasing your value to the team.

Notes on teamwork

Integration into a team is often thought of as being willing to help others on the team, work long hours when needed, or be instantly available to answer questions from teammates. Much of this is true, but if you do all of those things, you still won't be highly regarded as a teammate.

Instead, your first responsibility to the team is to reliably deliver your work to the team. If you consistently deliver quality work on time, your team will be able to count on you. You will hold up your part of the team so that others on the team can concentrate on their work.

Think about the teams you've been on in the past. If Joe didn't deliver his work on time or if his quality was poor, the rest of the team had to worry about his work and spend time fixing it. Joe could have been available to answer questions or work long hours, but the truth was that you never considered Joe a strong member of the team.

When you don't deliver your work on time to your team or manager, it is tough to be considered an important part of the team and worthy of higher performance ratings. Having the right job skills for the work and delivering the work sets you up to exceed expectations.

How to learn about the team

Every team has a micro culture that reflects their unique ways of inter-acting. Each team has leaders—not necessarily the manager—and each team has its own social forms.

Because business is social, the best way to learn about your team is to set up individual meetings or lunches with each member on the team. The meeting can last a half hour and should focus on how best to work with the other person on the team. I would try and recommend meeting one-on-one with each team member; you get a better perspective of the team rather than meeting with two or more from the team.

Here are the subjects to capture from your team:

- **Their role on the team.** If everyone does the same function on a team, the intent here is to find out about their specialized area within the function. You are the expert in.... If they perform a single function on a team, then learn about the function they perform.

- **Their inputs and outputs.** Every person on a team has a different view about where they get their work, how they do the work and how they deliver their work to their customers. Answering this question can also help you identify stakeholders and customers that may not be as apparent from the organization chart.

- **How best to work with them.** Since you need to integrate into the team, it is better to find out how best to work with each person on the team. Some people like e-mail questions and answers. Other people want you to walk over to their cubes and ask. Still others only like doing things in meetings. Some people want bullet point questions that are specific; others are perfectly content to have vague questions that can have brainstorming done to get to the real questions and answers. Your key here is to find the "fit" with each person so you can work well with him or her.

- **How best to work with your common manager.** Asking people how they best work with your manager can give you insight into how your manager operates on the team. To be clear, you are not looking for dirt on your manager; you want to understand how different people on your team see working best with your manager.

Learning about your team, figuring out their internal structure, and how to best work with individuals on your team is a critical goal for week two on your new job.

Know Your Workflow

With all this talk of learning about your manager, your team, how the organization is set up, and goals for the position, you'd think no work is getting done. Really, though, all of this is in addition to getting your work done. Your day job, after all, is completing tasks that get you closer to achieving your goals.

But how do you go about completing your tasks? That's done by following the workflow in the overall process of delivering your product to your customer.

Your job description talks "about the job"

When preparing for your interviews for this job, you most likely looked at the job description, looking for clues as to whether or not the job was a good fit for you. In the job description, you saw job skills, educational experience, certifications, and soft skills like teamwork that were requirements for the job.

But job descriptions don't tell you how to do the job, just what the job is about.

Workflow is "how to do the job"

When you sit down at your desk to accomplish something, you can't use the job description to guide you in your work. That is because job descriptions don't have the "how," only the "what."

Hopefully, in your meetings with your manager or your team, you were given a workflow diagram that says to start at "A" and end up at "Z." Hopefully, you were able to work with your manager and team and determine that you are responsible for steps "H through M" on the workflow diagram and were given access to the resources to accomplish those steps.

I say hopefully because the reality is that many companies do not do a good job of documenting how the work gets done. Managers, for good reasons, don't know all the steps for how their employees get the work done. Even when all of the steps are documented in a workflow, it doesn't mean the documentation matches how the work really gets done.

Yet, your success or failure in getting work done requires you to know the workflow. Getting the workflow wrong means making mistakes. Not that people need to be perfect, but making plenty of mistakes is disconcerting when you're starting out on a new job. Following the workflow means that you can confidently do the work and deliver meaningful results.

The question is this: What's the real workflow? Is it the one document-ed on the corporate? The one in the three-ring binder? The one that Joe verbally shared with you? The one Mary said was the way to do the work? Or a combination of all of them?

It is rare that you can point to one source as being the "right" one for doing the work. The documentation can be nailed, yet still not reflect the internal workings of the team.

Assume nothing

A key to success in your new role is getting the workflow down; getting repetitions in the workflow so that the workflow can be second nature to you. Just like training camp in sports, you practice and practice so that when the game day comes, you don't have to think about what you are doing. You just run the receiving route in football, snag the grounder in baseball, or don't think about your swing in golf.

So how do you know which workflow is right? Well, you don't. You can't assume that whatever workflow is given to you is the right one; you can only trust and verify. Even if the baseline workflow is right, there are usually too many variations of what you are working on to get all the permutations off of the baseline.

In short, you need to build a baseline workflow and then verify it as you go. Take the process, follow it to the letter to get some work done, then go back and review what worked, what could have worked better and what needs changing. Once you document that, you do the work again. Then look at the same things all over again. This is circular, of course, and iterative. But unless you build a baseline workflow, you have no reference point to change.

Getting the baseline workflow

Many good companies will have some or all of their workflows docu-mented. The workflows are often not maintained over time, so you shouldn't immediately assume they are true. But, at least there is something down on paper to look at and to add to and subtract from.

Most of the time, there is no documentation. Instead, we hand down our processes verbally, like the ancients preserving their history through oral documentation. This is why layoffs are so devastating to companies—how the work is done is lost through the people laid off and gone.

When there is no documentation, you need to document the process for yourself. There is no way you will remember all of the different ways of doing something unless you are working on a very simple process. When you are new to the department or the company, there is too much information to remember. Only when you write it down either on paper or in an electronic document will you have the ability to go back to it for reference and improvement.

Here's what you need to get documented:

- **The inputs to your work.** Requests come from somewhere for you to do work. It could be phone calls, e-mails, electronic or paper requests, or a variety of other inputs. What you are trying to do here is capture all of the different places that you can receive work—so you don't miss requests and fail on that work.

- **What you do with the requests for the work.** Does the request go into some system? You build a spreadsheet? You go give a patient a shot? Here is how you do your work from beginning to end.

- **Your output.** How is your work documented when complete? Does it go into some system? Noted in a log? Does a ticket get completed? Is a patient's medical record updated? When your task is completed, how do you know it is completed?

While this sounds simple, it can get complicated. Most of us do not deal with single requests or even requests of the same type. We may work on ten different types of requests—and all of them need documentation.

Once you have how your work is done documented, take the documentation out for a spin. When you get your request for work, did it come from where you expected? Did it have the right stuff for you to do your work?

Then, when you do your part, did you have the right access to do your job? The right tools to complete the work? Did you have all the steps in your baseline documentation?

Finally, when you completed your work, was your delivery to your customer right? Could you update everything needed correctly?

Your baseline workflow won't be right

With good documentation—and especially with little or no documentation—your baseline workflow will not be correct. Don't expect it to be. Don't get frustrated when it isn't. Just get the information down on your documentation and build a continuous feedback loop into your documentation.

A great technique for helping get your workflow right is to document what you have and then go ask a teammate about it. You are doing this to make sure "you get this right," but really what you are doing is trying to get it right and find out everything that's missing. When people tell you how something works, they give you what they think is complete information.

Then, when you go back to them and repeat back to them what you have, they will say something along the lines of "Well, that's right, but we also have this other place where we get work from and what you have doesn't apply." That is your big clue that what you have documented isn't close to enough.

I had a manager once who said, "They don't know what they don't know." That's your position here. Despite your job skills, previous experience, and gung-ho attitude, you don't know where all the inputs are coming from and all the systems to help you do your job. This is especially true if you are starting work at a new company.

So you need to look for those clues, detective-like, that will tell you that you need more information about how to do something for your work. Then add to your documentation. Building out your documentation will help you learn faster and get productive quicker.

The importance of prototyping your work

There is a fear among the newly hired of looking stupid at work because they don't know how something is done in this department or company. It is a dangerous fear because people don't ask questions about something because this is what makes them "stupid." The problem is that when you don't ask questions, you don't learn how something is done.

A great way around this fear is to prototype your work. Take a small sample of what you have done and go get feedback from your team, co-worker, or manager. If something is 10% complete, go ask about the 10% that is complete. Here's what you should ask about when prototyping your work:

- **Is the work in the right format?** You think the outline should be created in Microsoft Word because that's what you did in your old company. No, in this company, the outline should be written in PowerPoint. Why? It's the way it is done here.

- **Is the work at the right level of detail?** Are bullet points enough for people to understand? Or do we need explanations along with the bullet points to explain what we mean? Can we say three words and get the meaning because the three words are code for a hundred other words in the company? Or do we need to spell everything out? Can we use acronyms or not? All of these types of detail areas will help you improve the quality of what you are delivering.

- **Is the work complete enough?** Do we need to cover probable situations with less than a 5% chance of happening? What constitutes a worst-case scenario—and do we need to include it? Can we reference specifications, or do we need to spell them out here?

- **Is the work right for the audience (or customer)?** Is the language right for the customer? Will the next department understand it or is this too complicated? Is it too detailed for the Board of Directors or do we need to simplify what we are saying? Is a picture worth a thousand words, or is text the right way to go?

There are many reasons you want to prototype your work. First, you uncover hidden expectations about the work. People working in the department just know how they do something; this means they have assumptions about what you should already know. The reality is that you may have the work down cold—in your old company. But that may not be reality here. Prototyping your deliverable gives you the opportunity to uncover these assumptions very early in the process so you can correct them.

Second, you have time to recover. If you are doing something that isn't at the level it needs to be, you will find out early in the process and get to correct it. If you wait until the day something is due and proudly show off your work, you may find it rejected for many different reasons—by which point you have no time to recover from this. Plus, the rejection sets a poor mark on your early performance and that is difficult to overcome.

Third, you uncover more about the process while you are going through it. You can show your 10% off to your manager and your manager will casually ask if you've cleared what you've done with Joe. Well, you never were told, nor is it documented, that you should clear this with Joe. Think if you needed three approvals before you really completed your work and never got them because you didn't know. Prototyping allows you to get feedback openly while you are going through the process.

Fourth, you get variations on the process. "Oh, in this case, you also have to get input from Mary." "This is great, but when you are doing this for the Smith Corporation, they also require that you document this in Word, not just PowerPoint." "When it is Doctor Smith and it is this type of diagnosis, you also have to page him with the results." Getting all of these variations, or options, is the collective intelligence of the team that most often is not documented.

Finally, prototyping your work means you need to explain what you did to someone else. This gets you learning how to do things faster since explaining what you did requires you to figure out how to explain it. When we're on these short time frames to get up to speed and productive in a department, the document, explain, update document, and explain over again gives us a faster method of learning on the job.

If you think of prototyping as testing feasibility, it means you are testing what you are doing against your assumptions and documentation. And then filling in the holes along the way.

Workflow, as you can see, is this minefield that needs to be crossed so that you can do your work without thinking about how you do your work. It is tough to do because companies will often have poor, little, or no documentation about how the work gets done. Then you, as the Cubicle Warrior, need to re-create the workflows.

There is a longer-term benefit to documenting, prototyping and ex-plaining our work to others besides getting productive faster. The benefit is that we end up being in a great position to see what needs improving in the workflows. You already built the documentation. You can observe where things work well in the process and where they work poorly. This, after some experience, gives you the right perspec-tive on how to change a process to make it better. That creates value to your work.

Follow-up from Week One

One of the quickest ways to differentiate yourself from others is by following through on issues that are still outstanding and getting them to resolution. A big reason for doing a weekly review after starting your new position is to identify issues that need follow through the next week. What you don't want to do is not follow through on issues until week four and then not be able to do your work. Then you go to your manager and your manager wonders why it took you so long to bring the issue up.

So creating your follow-up list during the weekly review each week is a critical task for you to complete. For week two, what should your follow-up list look like?

Follow-up on your old job

One of the tasks you completed before starting your new job was working with your manager to define what "done" meant in your old job. You did this so that there were bright lines around what you would complete and what you would not complete as part of the transition to your dream job.

Perhaps you've gotten bogged down on some transition issues from the old job. Now is the time to really focus and wrap those issues up. If it means extra hours to get the work done, it is a good choice to make in this case. If it means the bright lines of your old commitments are not as bright, perhaps it is time to have a professional discussion with your old manager about the commitments each of you made to each other for what was to get done.

Updating your current manager about the work you are doing for the old job is also important for a couple of reasons. First, it will give your manager a sense of the availability you have for learning on the new job. If both your new manager and your old manager agreed on the work you still needed to do on the old job, it provides a good status report of where you are in the process.

Second, if the work is going over the bright lines of the agreement, you and your manager have the ability to push back on the work being done. This is why it is critical for you to get the agreement from your old manager on what you need to complete to get yourself to "done" in the old job. Without this agreement, you get a nagging overhang of work from the old job and never get to closure so you can move on.

Perhaps, instead, you haven't heard from your old group or your old manager. Or your dream job is with a different company. Week two is the week to give a courtesy call back to the person who took over doing your work and ask if there are any questions that need answering or any context that needs providing. Helping that person to get clarity about the work you were doing will help them complete their work effectively without wondering if they really got all the information they needed.

If the person who took over your work is fine with what they are doing, it's worth a call to your old manager to ask if there are any questions your old manager needs answering. It's a good idea to mention that you called the person taking over your work just to see if there were any questions. If asked, the follow through with the manager also gives you the ability to provide feedback on the person taking over your work.

Each of these calls builds a bridge back to the old group but, quite frankly, is rarely done. Something as simple as two phone calls will provide you great appreciation for the effort. Plus, each will remember your follow-through going forward. After all, your next manager might be the person taking over your work right now.

Follow-up on access issues

Access is getting the corporate resources so you can do your job. Access to computer systems, buildings and hardware can be vexing in some companies and simple in others. Without proper access to systems to do your work, you won't have the ability to complete your work effectively.

Follow through phone calls to the appropriate people and updating of status with your manager is appropriate here until you get the right access.

Follow-up on Goals

During your weekly review, you took a hard look at your goals, both the department and personal goals. Often, you will need clarification about how to achieve the goals, how to measure the goals, and who needs to work with you on the goals.

The sooner you get to clarity on your goals, the sooner you can take active steps to achieve them. So meet with your manager about your clarifying questions and get your answers.

You may still not get everything about the goals this week; just keep making progress on clarifying and validating your goals and measurement systems.

Follow-up on Organization

As part of your weekly review, you created a list of clarifying questions regarding the roles and responsibilities of the department and team. When you explain your view of the roles and responsibilities and ask your clarifying questions, you convey your understanding of how things work in the department and what you still need to learn.

Follow-up on Administrivia

If you've provided reporting to your manager, such as status reports or responses by e-mail, now is the time to check to see if the information is the right level of detail for your manager.

Following through on these issues gets issues resolved quicker, clarifies your thinking, and establishes you as a person who is organized and thorough—a great reputation to build early in your new job.

Weekly Review—Week Two

The weekly review this week focuses on the follow-up still needed from last week as well as our new activities this week on our dream job. Let's look at each one.

Week One follow-up. Depending on the type of organization you have joined, you could have no follow-up needed from the first week's work or plenty still on your list to complete.

In my mind, the number of items needing work on the list this week from the first week says a lot about the organization you are now working for. If you have properly followed through with your portion of the work and there are still plenty of items needing completion from the team or company resources, it should tell you that you will continuously need a "waiting for" list that you regularly review.

If, on the other hand, you had items on your list that needed work and that work is now complete, it tells you that you have a more competent organization that gets things done with relatively little follow-up. You still need the "waiting for" list to track outstanding work, of course, but the efficiency of the organization will help tremendously in supporting your work.

Notes from the team meetings. After getting situated with your manager in Week One, the big effort this week outside of completing tasks was to get to know your team. Now is the time to go through your notes from your individual discussions with your team members to ensure you understand their roles on the team, their inputs and outputs to their work, how best to work with them and your gleanings from them about how best to work with your common manager.

You are getting first impressions of how to evaluate your team, both in the roles they play on the team and how well they do their work.

By meeting with and working through how best to work with a particular person on the team, it should now be easier to see the interrelationships between the team members. Who is the natural leader on the team? Who is the "subject matter expert" in each area? Who does the team listen to the most when it comes time to choose a direction? How much does the manager defer to the knowledge of the team members? All of these interactions speak to the social structure of the team and you need to determine how you fit into that social structure.

You should also take some time in this weekly review to make some preliminary determination of how you add value to the team. What is it about your job skills, soft skills, or other knowledge that will give you a unique, compelling role on the team?

Building a preliminary view of how you add value to the team gives you some time to test your thoughts, try them out, and modify them as you go along. But the end game, identifying your unique value to your team, is necessary and critical for your ongoing success in any position.

Knowing your workflow. The second week on your dream job pushes you to complete tasks, meet the people you need for completing your work, and take you through your workflow. Thus, you are getting a good look at the process you need to follow to complete your work.

How's that working out? Is the process simple and easy to follow? Or is it convoluted, twisting, and opaque? Just as in the first week where you needed to explain your organization in your own words to increase your understanding, so here you need to write down your work process flow. By writing it down, you will quickly identify what you think you know and what you don't know.

Identifying where you have the process down cold and where you don't will allow you to build questions that will need answering in the next week so that your effectiveness in getting your work down goes up. You should identify the question about the workflow as well as the person to ask to get your answer.

Workflow also gives you perspective into the organization. Are the processes even identified, right or wrong? Or is everything stored in the heads of your team where the processes are just "known?" Do the processes have variations and exceptions identified? If they do, they are easy to validate. If they don't, you don't know what you don't know and will bump into the exceptions—and do them wrong.

The other subject to look at when it comes to workflows is a qualitative one: based on your experience, how simple, clean, and efficient does the workflow look? I'm not recommending that you go out there and start to suggest changes to how the work is done just yet, but you should have a gut feel for how work is done in your new organization.

Update your goals for the job. Do the goals you laid out for this job before you took it still work? How well is the job fitting into the goals?

It is still early to judge the job as great or poor, but constantly looking at your goals for the work against how the new job is going will give you a solid benchmark to use as you move along in the job.

Talk to your family about your new job. Of course, you and your family will have talked about your job in the first two weeks. But this section of the weekly review asks for feedback from them since you started your dream job. Is your stress up or down since you started? Are there any other changes in your behavior to them that they have noticed? When you share with them what you are doing, do they understand it? Are you able to explain it to them clearly, showing you understand it well enough?

Different people go through different emotions when they start a new job; everyone is unique. The point is not to get to feel some specific emotion or set of emotions at a particular point on the new job. The point is to have your family and you notice how you have changed since you took the job.

If your stress is way up compared to before you took your dream job, what's causing it? Or, if your stress is way down, what's different about this new job that it keeps your stress levels low?

Understanding your emotional state as you work through a new position helps you catch poor behaviors early, allows you to adapt to your emotional changes faster, and gives you greater peace of mind having identified how your emotions have changed.

5 | Week Three

Stakeholders Show You Success

As we move through the first 30 days in your dream job, we've continued to move your circle of contacts out. The first week, the focus was on the manager. The second week, the focus was on your team. In this third week, we shift focus to our stakeholders.

Stakeholders are people who have a vested interest in your work, but are not the people receiving your work (your customer). Your team members are both customers of your work and have a vested interest in your work and are stakeholders. So is your manager.

What I want to focus on here, though, is understanding who your stakeholders are outside of your team and manager. These are the people who know and understand your customers, but are not your customer.

For example, I managed a group that produced metrics that were included in reports that were given to internal customers. The customers worked with my group to develop the reports, were given presentations about how the metrics were determined and calculated, and had input to ensure the metrics were meaningful to their organization.

While the customers received direct input, there were other departments that had a strong interest in the reports, the metrics, and the results. The reason was that these departments interacted with the customer department. They wanted to know how our mutual customer was viewing services given to them. These other departments, while not having a say in how the reports were developed and delivered, nevertheless had a distinct, vested interest in knowing the results.

These are stakeholders.

While stakeholders do not have the same influence as customers, especially paying customers, they are powerful allies or enemies in supporting your work. Stakeholders can often limit the changes you can make to processes or products, veto new initiatives by withholding support, or use their influence with your customers to make life easier—or miserable—for you. Stakeholders can also give you great insight and different perspectives about your customers that can really help your work.

So stakeholders are important to identify, meet with, and establish great working relationships with as you do your work.

Identifying stakeholders

If you walk up to someone on your team and ask who the stakeholders are for your work, you are liable to get a blank stare. People don't think of stakeholders as a "category" of people like they do with "customers."

Instead, you need to ask different types of questions to determine the stakeholders for your work. "Who should I talk to about this work before I present this to the customer?" is a great question to ask. "Oh, you need to meet with John Smith so that he knows what's in it before the customer gets your work." That's a stakeholder.

Or, "Who would be surprised if our customer asked them about our work?" Nothing like blindsiding someone, right? That's a stakeholder.

You are looking for people who will influence your work, be questioned by customers about your work, or can help shape the work to better meet the needs of your customers.

Sometimes, you can easily see stakeholders from an organizational chart. You can infer that if you are delivering software improvements to the billing department, it might be a good thing to inform the accounts receivable department about the improvements so there are no surprises.

But, more often than you'd think, formal departments and organizational charts do not easily identify stakeholders or process flows. Instead, they are the informal organization that is only known through experience and making mistakes. Mistakes you'd want to avoid.

This is the person three departments over who has no formal or informal connection to your work—but used to work with your customer and the customer calls this person before doing anything with your work.

This is the person who should have a brief review of your work before presenting it because that person and your customer ride the bus together every morning and your stuff is bound to come up.

These are the three other managers who are on your level who can influence your common manager about the direction your work is taking. And if you don't, you won't be able to take the direction or advocate for your change.

Stakeholders will stay hidden unless you specifically ask questions about who they are, or who influences the work, or who it would be smart to show this work to before giving it to the customer.

And once you find a stakeholder, a great question to ask when you meet with them is "who else should see the work before presenting it to the customer?" Your stakeholder will often have the business network that your team and manager don't have to know who else has influence.

Few people ask those questions before delivering work to a customer and they get burned when the stakeholder wasn't consulted. And since business is social, you've put up a black mark on this stakeholder about your work.

Not a good way to start. So identifying stakeholders by asking these leading questions to your team and your manager will help flesh out who the stakeholders are for your work.

Stakeholders build your internal business network

Stakeholders are important for a different reason: they build your business network. Now, your business network is the group of people you can call on to bounce ideas off of, look for mentors, and test your thoughts on how to change something—or look for a different job. The bigger your business network, and the better your reputation in it for delivering quality, the larger your base of people to support you.

This support is important on many different levels. For example, let's say you start your dream job, have done well integrating yourself with the stakeholders on your job, and then your manager changes in a re-organization. Happens all the time. But this new manager has a style that is difficult to work with. If your manager tries to undercut you in performance reviews or meetings, who is there to protect your interests? Your stakeholders. They can push back on a poor manager because they know your work.

Or, consider a change you want to make to a process or policy. Working with all the stakeholders not only allows you to garner support for the change, but you'll find out all the objections that need overcoming through talking through the change with your stakeholders. In short, you'll build a better change and get the support of people who have a vested interest in the change.

When you don't understand something in the company, stakeholders can act as subject matter experts in their area and give you the right context for what you don't understand. Because you have reached out to them and offered your help, they will most likely help you in understanding something that they are good at doing. This improves your business knowledge, builds your business relationship with people, and shows that you value their input.

Just as your team moves on to other jobs thereby giving you contacts in other areas of the company or industry, so do stakeholders. Maintaining relationships with stakeholders even after they are no longer a direct stakeholder to your work builds your business network to other areas of the company or industry. Having a large, interactive business network opens up opportunities to you that you would never see or hear about without this investment in stakeholders.

Know your stakeholders like you know your team

Just as you need to know how to communicate with your team, know their strengths and know how best to work with them, so too the need to do the same thing with your stakeholders.

You won't necessarily meet with every stakeholder during this week—or even know all of the stakeholders out there—but the sooner you can identify, meet with, and understand your stakeholders, the faster you will learn about the company and the job.

So break out the questions you used to interview your team and start using them with your stakeholders. The one difference in your approach to stakeholders compared to your team is that your team is a finite number of people. There are five or seven or whatever number of people on your team.

Stakeholders don't have finite numbers. There can be five stakeholders—or fifty. It depends on the work and the customer for your work. Plus, your manager or your team won't necessarily know who all the stakeholders are—because they don't do this in their job!

Thus, unlike your team, you need to ask the stakeholder you are working with "whom else should I speak with about my work?" By asking this question or one like it, you can build your network with people completely independent of your manager and team.

Evaluate Your Team

When you are in Week Three, it is time to start doing some evaluation—judgments, if you will—of your team and manager. This may seem drastic; after all, you've only been on your dream job for a couple of weeks and already you are doing an evaluation of your team.

But haven't you done that all along? Every time you meet with a team member, whether in a team meeting or in a one-on-one situation, haven't you evaluated that person, their capabilities and how well you can work with them? Sure you have, you just haven't formalized the thinking around the evaluations.

So what we are doing here in this portion of your journey is providing a formal approach to evaluating your team and, in the next section, for doing so with your manager.

Why you need to evaluate your team

Succeeding in your new job is a combination of delivering your tasks and meeting your goals, integrating with your team, and providing a unique value that only you bring to a team. You want the unique value so that you aren't simply expendable if and when times get tough.

The first reason to evaluate your team is to determine if you are integrating well into the team. Since your hiring is disruptive to the team, even if you are a fabulous and welcomed addition, you need to determine how integration is going.

The second reason to evaluate the team is to determine the team assets. These are the specialties that each team member has that bring value to the team. Knowing each person's assets helps you determine where to get advice and who to work with on projects to best match resources to the problems at hand.

The third reason to evaluate the team is to start determining where your unique value is to the team. Now, it could be that your unique value to your team was the reason your manager hired you for the job. It may be obvious what your unique value is to the team and the team sees this value in your work.

More often, the unique value you bring to the team is not so clear. If your manager or your manager's manager thinks of your group as a ubiquitous set of skills with each person performing the same work, it is easy to think of the function of the team as being very important—or worthless. In a layoff situation where only part of the team is released, having duplicate skills and no unique value means your chances of getting laid off are very high.

So evaluating your team and then figuring out where your value is to the team is an important step and not one that can be casually considered. Getting to a unique value for your work on the team—and having the team and your manager recognize the unique value—is important for your long term success in your dream job.

The final reason to evaluate the team is to give yourself enough time to change direction or fix problems that you identify early on in the job hire so that your reputation doesn't morph into something bad.

This week is where you establish the baseline for your team—their strengths, weaknesses, decision making skills and how you can establish a unique value to the team. When you establish this baseline, you can now compare it to your impressions in future weeks and make adjustments to your approach to the team.

For example, you may think that you have identified a unique value to the team and start to use that in your work. Because you established a baseline this week about what that unique value is, you can now look at it during a weekly review and determine if it is the best value to bring to the team or if you should consider changing it.

Without this baseline evaluation, you will drift in your analysis, never settle on how best to work the team, nor figure out the best value to bring to the team. That diminishes the chance of success in your dream job.

What you need to do to evaluate your team is evaluate each person on the team and then evaluate the overall team and its ability to reach their business goals. Let's look at each area.

Evaluating a team member

One of the first ways to evaluate a team member is knowing how well they understand the business. It is one thing to know about your work and how to get it done, but another to understand the business. You can know code, but do you understand how the bank branch is run with the program code you produce? If you are a nurse, do you understand where the information you enter about a patient goes and how it is used?

Understanding the broader picture is useful in that you have a better connection to what you are doing and how it affects others in the business. Different team members, of course, will have different areas of the business they understand because of their interests or their work. But knowing you can go to John to find out about cash flows and to Mary about accounts receivable helps you know your resources in your work.

Another way to evaluate a team member is in knowing their unique value to the team. What is it they know best about the work? In my years as a manager, I've found that what people say they are best at doing isn't the best job skill they have. I don't know if it is because people think their strengths are different from what they are or if they just don't know. What I always did with my team was provide them with many different tasks to do and then discover which they did best—and their best rarely matched their stated best job skill.

So when you ask the person what unique value they bring to the team, listen carefully and then attempt to verify that what they say really is the unique value. You will know this because other team members ask this person for help using this unique value or that the team defers to this person's knowledge on a topic when they talk about it.

In addition, many team members will have more than one unique talent for the team. Just as in college, you many want to note that one of your team members has a "major" area where they are an expert and a "minor" area as well.

Knowing these areas in each of your team members helps you call on the right resources for the job or to answer your questions. These areas also tell you that the probability of your becoming the expert in an area already covered by a particular team member is smaller than finding one of your own.

Both the knowledge of the business and each person's unique value to the team relate to their knowledge of the work. An additional way to evaluate team members is through their work habits.

The particular work habits we're concerned about is knowing the best way to work with a person, whether the person consistently delivers their work, and if they consistently follow up on their commitments.

Knowing the best way to work with another individual simply smoothes the establishment of the relationship. If someone wants an e-mail to study and have a set meeting time to discuss something, that is very different from someone who simply wants you to walk over to their cube and ask them a question. Both achieve the goal, but the means to the goal are very different.

Walking over and interrupting a person who wants an e-mail and a quick meeting time will just irritate them. Likewise, sending an e-mail with your request and asking for a quick meeting time will make the person who wants you to just walk on over to their cube and ask your questions wonder why you don't want to get stuff done faster. What's all this meeting stuff, anyway?

So knowing how a person likes to get their work done—and, by the way, you knowing how *you* best work—is an important method of getting a good relationship going with your team.

The reason you want to establish this baseline with each team member on how they work is to see if how they operate is true in practice. I once had a manager, for example, who said, "Never walk into this office with a problem unless you have potential solutions!" So whenever I walked in with a problem, I also had a couple of solutions for us to pick from.

When it came time for my performance review, I was chastised for having a "know it all" attitude. How did I get this imaginary attitude? I always walked into my manager's office with potential solutions to problems just like he wanted me to do!

Well, the next time I had a problem—and even though I had a couple of potential solutions—I walked into the office and said that I really needed his advice on what to do. I had thought it through and through, but just didn't have potential answers. It was like sending a kid into a candy store. My manager could now triumphantly proclaim answers to problems and he could think of them himself and bless me with his wisdom!

Sure, he *said* he wanted solutions to problems walking in the door (pretty standard approach), but the *reality* was he wanted to pontificate, ponder, and offer his own solution to my problem. So I never offered a solution again.

Without this baseline of how people say they operate compared with how they actually operate, you won't have the right approach to working with your team.

The next characteristic you want to determine about your team is whether or not they deliver on their work. Does Mary always deliver her work on time and with great quality? Yes—a great person to pair with on projects because you can count on her to do her part. Does John deliver his work on time? No, he's always in crisis mode and the work he does is never right the first time he delivers it. Would you want to work with John on a project if that's how he operates? Have fun fixing all his work and taking time away from you trying to get your work done?

Delivery of their own work is the greatest gift a teammate can give you to show teamwork. You need to know if you can count on a person to deliver their work so that you can have confidence in the person you are working with.

The next work habit you want to recognize in your team is their ability to follow through to completion. While this is similar to delivering their work on time, it is more about how many times you need to follow through with them to get what you asked them to do.

If you ask one of your teammates for some information, do they capture it, tell you when you'll have the information back, communicate any problems they encounter that might affect their delivery of the information and deliver it to you without your ever having to follow up? Or do you have to ask the person their status on their deliverable to you? Do you ask them how they are doing the day before the due date and they ask you what it was, again, you were looking for?

Some people have their task management system down cold and you never need to follow up with them about something they agreed to do. Others need following up every day to make sure they stay on track.

Which person would you rather work with on a project? How much time will you have taken away from you to complete your work when your follow-up list with people is a mile long?

Knowing the work habits of your team, then, has a significant impact on your ability to produce work efficiently and effectively.

The final consideration of each team member is his or her leadership impact on the team. Some people think that leadership is only for managers, but that's not the case. Leadership can show through anyone on any team even if they are an individual contributor on the team.

Leadership on a team isn't something on an organizational chart. Instead, it must be inferred by the actions on the team. When John speaks, does everyone listen? When Mary suggests a solution to a problem is that the one that's used? When John and Mary both agree with a direction is that the direction the manager takes in a meeting?

Within a team there are leaders and there are followers, neither of which is bad or good. The roles simply exist on every team. As a new person on a team, you need to understand who plays these roles. The reason is simple: when you are new on a team, you are, by default, a follower. You don't have credibility just yet because you don't have a track record like the current team members.

If you want to get stuff done on the team, the first thing you have to do is understand whom to influence. If John and Mary are the leaders on the team and if your first shot at contributing to the team is going against what John and Mary want, it is far more upsetting to the team—maybe fatal—than building on what John and Mary are saying to make a better solution.

Truly great teams shift leadership around based on expertise needed in certain areas. You can have an overall project; for example, where the solution to issues in accounts payable almost always come from Mary because it is her area of expertise. She knows the answers and everyone else knows she knows the answers. John, on the other hand, provides leadership in the accounts receivable area because that's his area of expertise. In the meantime, Pat has the leadership in the billing area because Pat has that area down cold.

Management defers to these leaders on the team for each of the areas and the team defers to each team member's area of expertise because they have the confidence from the proven track record of each person. These teams are fabulous to work on—but you, as a new person, have much to prove before you can become a leader in your area.

Knowing how the leadership on the team plays out is critical to both integrating yourself on the team and having an ability to move what you need done forward on a team.

Evaluating a team

Knowing how to evaluate a person on a team is different from knowing how to evaluate a team. Just as evaluating one person on a sports team is different from evaluating the sports team in relation to the rest of the league.

When you evaluate an entire team, there are three good starting questions:

First, "How well will the team advance the business goals given to them by their manager?" Here you look at the entire team and see if the right roles are available on the team to reach the goals. If, for example, you have to provide support for five different applications, do you have at least one role expert in each of the five applications? If the answer is yes, you have a shot. If you only have a role expert in four of the five, you are at risk for reaching the goal.

Now, goals have stories for how to reach them and each person on the team has a role in the story. If the goal is to increase inventory turnover by 5% by stocking more of what is selling well and less of what is selling less, who on the team is determining what is selling well and what is selling less? If you can answer the "Who has this role to meet the goal?" with someone on your team, you have a team that is set up right to meet the goal.

The second critical question to ask yourself is "How well do the team and manager relate to each other?" The manager-team relationship is both authoritarian due to the organizational structure as well as a social relationship because business is social.

The manager-team relationship covers the entire spectrum of behavior depending on the people on the team and the manager's management style. Is the team self-sustaining without much manager input? Then there is a great fit with a hands-off management style. Put a "check every detail" manager in place with a self-sustaining team and you'll have conflict.

Does the manager decide the direction or does the manager listen to input from the team? Does the manager give direction to the team and the team then follows through? Or does the team ignore the advice and just move on?

What you are hoping for is a "trusted advisor" relationship between the team and the manager where the manager trusts what the team is saying and acts on it. And the team trusts what the manager is saying and acts on it.

That rarely happens, however. The closer to the "trusted advisor" relationship the manager and team have, the more productive the team will likely be—and you as well. The more dysfunctional the manager-team relationship, the more conflict-ridden and unproductive the team—and you with it.

So the working relationship between the manager and team is critical to the overall success, of which you are a part, of the team reaching their goals.

Finally, the third question to ask is "What is the reputation of the team to other managers?" This is human nature at work: the better the team, the less interference from outside parties to the team. The worse the team's performance, the more outside forces pile on to fix your problems whether they are affected by your work (stakeholders) or not. People blame events on others and, if your team has a poor reputation, you'll have plenty of blame directed at you.

In addition, teams with good reputations with other managers are, logically, higher valued in the organization. When it comes time for a layoff, platinum team reputations outweigh poor reputations. The teams with the poorest reputations, deserved or not, won't be around when layoffs come. Or, to look at the stellar reputation in a more optimistic light, great teams get more great work that continues to reinforce the great team reputation.

One of the best ways to gauge the reputation of your team with other managers is ask the stakeholders of our work their opinion about your team. Does the team deliver good work? What are the strengths of the team from their viewpoint? What areas can your team improve in the eyes of the stakeholder?

Since you are new on the team, you can help solidify the view of your team's reputation in one direction or another. Knowing your team's reputation, though, will tell you a lot about what needs doing to make the team better.

There are enough sports stories out there that hit the theme of "great individuals do not necessarily make a great team." We've all seen everyone on a team think they are stars and yet the overall effectiveness of the team drops to zero.

So, for us in our dream job, we can't just evaluate the members of our team and think the work is done. We also need to determine the effectiveness of our team so we have a baseline to evaluate.

Evaluate Your Manager

By now, in your third week of your dream job, you have had multiple opportunities to interact with your manager. These interactions would include face-to-face conversations, e-mail, meetings, and business social interactions with your team.

One of your keys to success is having a great working relationship with your manager. Your manager, after all, has the greatest influence on your career right now through performance reviews, pay raises, promotion opportunities and influencing your work reputation with other managers.

This week, a key goal is to do an evaluation of your manager. Just as you evaluated your team, the same need is there to evaluate your manager, and for all the same reasons.

Five ways to evaluate your manager

The first way to evaluate your manager is **the management "style."** Style is a broad term about how a person goes about managing. There are many different styles; as well, there are many combinations of style. Let's look at a few of the major management styles.

The Dictator. In this style, the manager makes all the decisions. There is little discussion about the options and once it is clear what The Dictator wants to do, the team essentially has no choice but to follow that lead.

The Benevolent Dictator. Here, the manager will listen to input from the team, but the manager will still make the final decision. The decision, however, is based on what is best for the team and the business.

The Democratic Manager. Here you get to a level where the team not only gets input into a decision, but can actually make them. Democracies, of course, are messy, but this style gets issues out and allows for consensus within the team. I like to characterize this as a democracy, but, in the end, the manager always has one more vote than the combined team members.

The Micro Manager. This management style is where everything has to go through the manager for approval. Want to talk to another organization? You have to ask first. Want to go to a meeting where you are needed for input? The manager needs inviting too whether the manager attends or not. Want to show your work to a stakeholder to get feedback? The manager needs to see the work first. There is attention to detail and then there is *attention to detail.*

The Anything Goes Manager. This is a manager who doesn't want to engage in the management process for whatever reason.

There are other styles, of course, but the intent here is to show you some broad categories that you manager fits into based on your interactions with him or her. Each of these management styles has its strengths and weaknesses in any given situation. If a manager, for example, is brought in to bring about fast change in a department that isn't working well, then being a Dictator is probably necessary to get the changes needed off the ground and moving.

On the other hand, a well-established, high-performing, collaborative team would fall apart with a Dictator for a manager. All the good team dynamics would get dictated away by this type of manager.

So your evaluation, then, starts with what type of team you are working with on your dream job. Then you need to identify the management style of your manager. Finally, you make some judgments about the manager's style and the appropriateness of the style with the team.

Your second evaluation is **your relationship with your manager in a one-on-one situation.** When you go to your manager's office or cube, how does the relationship work? Is it one where you are the servant visiting the king? Is it collaborative? Are the interactions focused on making decisions, improving the work and doing what's right for the department?

After three full weeks on the job, has the manager dropped out of existence? Or is there a right balance between supporting your efforts in your work and leaving you alone to do the work?

The keys in your relationship with your manager are your ability to communicate your support needs to get your work completed and understanding what makes an "outstanding" delivery of work on your part. You want an "outstanding" performance review rating, so what does "outstanding" mean for each and every deliverable? Without the ability to communicate your support needs and understanding what "outstanding" work is, you won't succeed in the new job.

The third method of evaluating your manager comes from **the conduct in meetings.** Meetings are the "public" work of different groups of people coming together to make a decision about something. Meetings allow for a give and take among positions, tasks to assign, and decisions to make.

How your manager handles meetings that he or she runs is a good indicator of how well your manager is in the job. Does the manager have an agenda for the meeting? Does his or her leadership guide the meeting? How is dissent handled to positions your manager takes? How does your manager close out a decision by assigning work?

But managers don't just run meetings; they participate in them as well. As a participant, does your manager come prepared to the meeting to get things done or does he or she just wing it? Does your manager keep to the topics on the agenda or does your manager wander all over the place, unable to make a decision? Does your manager offer respectful dissent or does your manager attack others for their views?

It is fairly well known that people who work for corporations spend an inordinate amount of time in mostly unproductive meetings. If your manager is one that moves the meeting to productivity and decision-making, it will help you and your team accomplish their goals. If your manager doesn't move your goals through when in meetings by making decisions and contributing positively to the conversation, then you and your team will have a harder time reaching your goals.

The fourth method of evaluating your manager is **how your manager works with his or her peers** and the culture of the management team. Just as you are part of a team working towards common goals, so too is your manager part of a management team working toward common goals.

The importance of understanding your manager's position within the management team and the reputation your manager has will make work easier or harder for you. If your manager has a fabulous reputation for getting things done, then you'll have to get stuff done but will most likely get more support and help to do so because your manager can ask for resources and help.

If your manager's reputation is not that great with the rest of the management team, your manager will be questioned about every request. Critical scrutiny will be given to any overruns on the budget. Requests for additional help will be evaluated in light of adding resources to marginal managers. It is simply harder to work in an environment that is constantly critical of the work you and your manager are doing.

Now, you are part of your manager's team. Perhaps some of the reason you were hired was to increase the deliverables of the department and improve the quality of the work. In other words, your work is part of what drives the reputation of the manager with the manager's peers. One can't blame the manager for everything when you contribute to the manager's reputation.

But knowing where your manager fits in the team gives you another indication of how well your work will be received over time in the department. Plus it will tell you what needs doing in the department to support the manager.

The fifth method of evaluating your manager is by observing **how well the manager removes roadblocks** for getting the team's work done. If you are asking for support to get work done and so are your coworkers, how often is the support done? Does the support happen all the time (most likely not)? Is there reasonable questioning by the manager before support is offered (why can't you do this work without the support)?

Usually, when asking for support, you need to build a reasonable case for the support from the manager. The manager needs to go ask other people for help. The manager wants assurances that asking for support won't damage the manager's reputation and waste everyone's time. Plus the manager wants assurances that you really can't get the work done without the support—why is the work so beyond your capacity to accomplish?

When asking for support, then, it is not enough in your evaluation to say the manager did or did not get rid of the roadblocks for you and get the right type of support. When you do the evaluation, you need to ensure there was a case built for the support, the case was supported by facts, and the request was not an excuse to not do the work.

Once you know your initial view of how much support you can expect from your manager, you are now in a position to translate that into how much work you will accomplish. If you have a manager who offers great support, you will get more work done relative to a manager who doesn't supply great support. This makes sense; without support from management, work doesn't get done. It's just that too many people complain about management not helping without recognizing that the lack of support significantly impacts your career and job success.

There comes a time, in fact, where the complete lack of support from management about the work requires you to question the importance of the work to the company. Often, one of the first signs of an impending layoff is when you or your team no longer get support from management for your work. The absence of managerial involvement in the department means limited management resources no longer think your work is critical to their success.

This most likely won't happen when you first start—otherwise you would never have been hired. But it is important to get a baseline for your management support so that six months from now you can tell if that support is the same, better—or worse.

Your Management Goal: The Trusted Advisor

The early reading on your manager is important because it creates a baseline for your ultimate goal with your manager: become the trusted advisor. A trusted advisor is one where you can advocate your point of view for the business with your manager in a trusted environment. It's where you can say what needs saying and then once the decision is made, you both jump into the foxhole together regardless of whether or not your advice was taken.

The trusted advisor role is important on several levels. In order to get to this position with your manager, you have had to build a level of trust that warrants the trusted advisor role. This usually translates into a greater engagement in the work you are doing, giving you greater satisfaction with the role.

In addition, you can't get to a trusted advisor role unless you learn how to keep confidences. Keeping confidences—whether with your manager or with your coworkers—is a *Cubicle Warrior* skill. While it can feel great to spread whatever is said in the workplace, the smarter move is to keep the information to yourself.

Once you demonstrate you can keep confidences, you are more likely to hear confidential information—or at least better hints about it—than if you were not in the trusted advisor role. This gives you valuable insight into current conditions in the company and good hints at what is to come. This significantly improves your ability to adjust your work to match up with what is coming. And this includes finding a new job or knowing a lot more about how long a position lasts.

Finally, the trusted advisor role is rare. That rarity is rewarded through protecting your role in the organization more than others. This protection can put you in a different job, out of harm's way, long before bad things happen to your former group. This can put you into a better position to advance your career and help the company in a better role. All of these situations are helped through your role with your manager.

Now, it is not easy to get to this level of trust with your manager. It shouldn't. But without a baseline evaluation of your manager, management capabilities and manager's impact on the management team, you won't know how to go about getting to this type of role.

In addition, each manager responds—just like all people—to the situation at hand differently than does another manager. One manager wants the directness of your opinion. A different manager doesn't want ideas unless he invents them himself. A different manager wants to hear the implications of a decision while another doesn't care. Some want input and others just want you to do the work.

Without understanding how your manager makes decisions, what actions influence work and which don't, and how to go about improving your relationship with your manager, you will have a more difficult time succeeding. So understanding how your manager works is important to building the right relationship.

Weekly Review—Week Three

Here we are at the Week Three review. By now, you should have a good idea on how this works for the week and how to do the review. But let's make sure we get the highlights for the week down and see where you are in your dream job.

Stakeholders

You discover your stakeholders as you deliver your work. When going over your notes from your conversations with stakeholders, pay particular attention to two areas.

The first area is comments about your customers. What characteristics do your customers have that you might not know about? Here, characteristics about how they like the work delivered, formatted, or reviewed provide good hints on your ability to successfully engage with your customers.

The second area is to extract out areas of the work done previously by people who did your job who were successful—or failed. Both sides of the coin in this case are important. You want to continue doing what is successful. After all, your first goal should be "do no harm." The last person in the job did something correctly; make sure you continue what is considered successful.

It should be obvious that you want to fix what failed in the work in the position you are in. The purpose of the review here, though, is determining if the failure was due to the person doing the work before or if the failure stems from the system—the workflow, external processes, or some form of management failure.

If you suspect that the failure comes from these areas outside your control, you can fail just as well as the previous person in the position. Knowing these areas and validating the true causes of what didn't work will help you determine your success on the job.

Your Team

You spent a lot of time this week determining the effectiveness of your team. Plus the resources the team brings to the work. Your review should lay out your view of the strengths and weakness of the team you are on. In addition, you should work through your unique value that you bring to the team.

Your Manager

Your manager has tremendous influence on your job effectiveness and career. You've now spent three weeks with your manager—how is it going?

Do you understand the management style used by your manager? Can you determine how your manager makes decisions? Can you see yourself as a Trusted Advisor to your manager? Do you know when you approach your manager how to successfully get what you are asking for?

Most people leave their jobs because they don't like the manager. Better to understand this early to get a jump on this gig being great or a great waste.

Carryover

Of course, every week has some carryover of tasks to complete or that were not understood well. Make a list of these and follow through with them next week.

6 Week Four

Your Manager Is Your Most Important Customer

If you have had anything pounded into your head about business, it is that the most important person in business is the customer.

Ah, yes, the customer. The serious question is this one: who is your customer?

Your customers are *the people who accept the output of your work as an input to their work.*

Think about that for a moment. When you write up a report that shows results from something, you give it to someone. That someone is your customer.

If you look at the people you give your work to as your customers, who is the most important customer you have?

Your manager.

Yes, your manager is your most important customer. Your manager sees most of your work before it goes to the final person for delivery.

Your manager is the one who critiques the work, offers suggestions to improve it, and evaluates the work as part of your job performance.

But there are other, equally important, reasons for knowing that your manager is your most important customer. Let's look at them in some detail.

Your manager determines your pay raise and bonus

This is the heart of knowing your customer. Your manager has tremendous control and influence to determine your future earnings.

Consider performance reviews. Your manager is the person who determines your performance review rating. That rating is tied to your raise and bonus. The higher the performance review rating, the higher the pay raise and bonus. And don't discount even small differences in pay between different performance review ratings. Having a consistent pay raise of 3.5% from a higher performance review rating compared to one of 2.5% over the course of five years is a significant difference in purchasing power. That one percent per year is often the difference between keeping up with inflation or losing purchasing power.

Managers know the difference between people who work for them who get the fact that the manager is the most important customer and ones that think other people are the most important customers. Where it shows up is in the setting of the performance review rating and in calibration sessions where your work performance is defended—or not.

Getting better performance review ratings requires significant work, of course. But the very first attitude you need to have is that your manager is your most important customer. Taking care of the manager's work first, making sure the manager's work is done the way your manager—customer—wants it done, and doing high quality work for the manager goes a long way to improving your performance review rating.

This does not mean you simply nod yes every time your manager asks you about something or to do something. Good managers want your business judgment on issues and you should provide it. But it does mean that you should deliver what your most important customer wants after agreeing on what should be delivered.

Your manager is your biggest influence on your career right now

In addition to performance reviews, your manager has the ability to support or block your career choices in a company. Are you tired of working in a particular area and want a change? Your manager has to approve it. Do you want to build your job skills by working in a different job within the company? Your manager has to approve it.

Even if your manager is okay with your doing a job change within the department or the company, the manager can give the approval—but not follow up with the negotiations to get you the transfer.

Think about your desire to move to a different department within the company. You bring it up to your manager, your manager agrees, and tells you to go for it. Then the manager sits on his or her hands while you spin your wheels trying to get the transfer.

Contrast that with the manager approving your job change idea and then the manager going to the manager of the target department, talking through your desire to work in the department, offering your target manager a good review of your work, and then working with the manager to fill the opening by selecting you. Or making sure that when the next opening in the department comes along, you have the inside track on getting the open position.

There is a world of difference between simply approving some action and going out to advocate for it. That's influence.

It may be that you have a great manager and your manager would go advocate for you if you wanted the change. But your chance of getting the advocacy is higher if you understand that your manager is your most important customer and you've done the work to prove it.

Your manager can promote your personal brand in the company—or kill it

Your manager has great power to direct your work in a way that enhances your value to the company or hurts it. The problem for the employees of the manager is that the work opportunities are hidden until the manager assigns the work.

Consider, for example, a solid chunk of work comes to the manager to get assigned. The work is on the top project for the company. The manager then weighs who should get the work—knowing the outcome of the work also directly contributes or detracts from his or her standing within the management ranks. The manager is going to give the work not only to someone qualified to do it, but also to the person who understands that the manager is the most important customer.

Or consider when another manager comes to your manager asking for resources. Let's even say that the other manager comes to your manager and specifically asks for your help on some chunk of work. Your manager will accept the suggestion of you doing the work or not—but you will never know the answer to that because it was done as a private conversation requesting resources.

The work that is assigned has value both to the company as well as to the manager's reputation within the company. Your performance in doing the work will either help your standing within the department or it won't. And your manager is the one who decides how to assign the work.

I call this power of selecting work to assign as "leaving opportunities on the table." You never knew about the opportunity, could never show your work, and thus won't have the accomplishments you can show on your performance review. If you want to ensure that you have the maximum number of opportunities, doesn't it make sense to have your manager as your most important customer?

This is not some conspiracy theory about management and how they assign the work. Managers mostly want to do the right thing for their company and their employees. But it is much easier for a manager to do the right thing by the employee recognizing that their manager is their most important customer.

Know Your Customers

If you consider people who accept the output of your work, you will have several sets of customers.

The first group of people who are your customers are your peers on your team. You work with your team on tasks that the overall department will deliver to your manager or your other customers.

Then, finally, customers are those people to whom you deliver your work output.

There is something subtle here about delivery of your work. You deliver your work to people, or to a group of people. You don't deliver your work to some process, some system, or some other department within the business. You deliver your work to people.

This orientation to people is important for several reasons. First, it is easy to get caught up in technology—social media is the rage, but e-mail is just as technologically to blame—instead of dealing with people. E-mail, and other social media, is easy. It's easy to send, easy to deliver—and easy to blow relationships.

Technology separates us from people. Phone calls, where a large percentage of communication is lost due to not seeing the non-verbal clues from the other person, are bad enough but the rest of technology distances us from our social selves and the people we work with. Too many misunderstandings, too many disagreements, and too much time is wasted using technology to deliver our work.

So your customer isn't some process or some department. Your customer is "Jane" working in the next department and "Joe" who helps Jane do the work.

The second reason for the people orientation is that people are more engaged in the job when they know their work impacts people and not just processes. If I don't write the book, the publisher probably doesn't care. But the people who start out on new jobs, frustrated at not having guideposts and overwhelmed from information overload, do care—they just don't know yet about this book.

So my engagement in writing this book doesn't come from the publisher; instead, it comes from writing for the people who would love to have this kind of guide when they are starting out on a new job.

Connecting to people means that if you don't deliver your work right, Jane is going to take a hit on her job. And Joe won't be able to help her do her work. When you deliver your work right, Jane and Joe are grateful you are the one doing the work because you get it.

In delivering your work and looking for your customers, you need to drive that search to specific people. You want to personalize your work and not mask it in technology. And you want to have relationships with the people who are your customers because it engages you to do a better job with greater satisfaction.

You've identified your customers—now what?

Four questions to ask your customers

Once you have identified your customers, you want to start working with them. Your manager and your team may tell you all about your customers, but that doesn't mean you know everything about your customers. Plus, your customer will appreciate your asking a few questions to them because it shows you want to know their specific needs.

Here are the questions.

1. *What do they do with the output of your work?* It is surprising how many people don't understand what happens to their work once they hand it over. It is easy to simply deliver the work, chalk that up to another successful task finished, and to move on to the next task.

   But you can get great insights into both your work and what the customer does with your work by asking this question. Since the question is about what the customer does with your work, the question is more interesting to the customer. People talk about themselves; we should use that to our advantage.

   What the answer gives you is the ability to evaluate if you can do something different that increase the value of your work for your customer. Whether it is adding an entire module to something or reformatting the work so that it is done the way the customer uses your data, you can discover new and different ways to make your customer's experience better.

2. *What benefit does your work provide the customer?* Is your work output something they could never live without? Or is it some little section of a small report that no one looks at? You are evaluating the importance of what you do in the customer's eyes.

   Obviously, you want your stuff to be so important that the customer can't live without it. If that's the case, you want to make sure that all of your systems, processes, and task management are designed to deliver your work on time and with the highest quality. Any little glitch that happens preventing you from delivering your work to your customer will have a major impact on what they do.

   On the other hand, if your work is this little thing they get from you that they don't care much about, you want to find out how to make what you do more important to them. Are you close to something important that you could change? Are you supporting some process but need to get tied into a more important one? You want to be in a position where the customer can't live without your work. This question helps determine where you are in this range of importance of work.

3. *What are their suggestions for improving your work?* It is one thing to know the importance of your work and how your customer uses it. But quality of the work is a different issue altogether. This question gets to the quality of the work you and your team produce. Does your stuff come to them at the wrong time? Is it in the wrong format? Does it lack analysis? Could you tweak the information to help them?

   Quality of work is usually thought of as how "accurate" the work is that is delivered. But quality is also about the type of information provided, the consistency of the delivery and timing of the work. Quality issues usually means re-work on the customer's end, and it diminishes the importance of what you deliver.

   Asking how what you are supposed to deliver on the job could improve, especially if asked before you provide any deliverables so you can see past performance of the department, is a powerful way to begin building a partnership with your customer.

4. *What questions does your customer have about your work?* Just as many of us don't know what happens to our work after we deliver it, our customer often doesn't understand the hoops we go through to deliver our work to them.

   This is a great question to ask because you will often find that the portion of some deliverable you go through hoops to get isn't really important to them. I've asked this question and gotten into a conversation about what we do to deliver some part of our work and my customer has said it wasn't worth the hassle and don't do the work anymore! Now that's a great way to simplify your work—and make it easier for you to do as well.

Questions give you context

What is important about these questions is that the answers give you context into what your customer wants, what they say, why they think you are great and why they think the work needs improving. You can't get defensive about the answers, especially if you haven't yet done any work for them, but you want to see a relationship baseline with your customers.

Since this is often very early on in the relationship, your customer is also going to be far more social (read: polite) with you about the problems of the past because your customer will hope you will do the work better.

Even if the relationship is a good one, asking these questions, getting the answers, and then having some of their suggestions built into what you do with your work will show your customers that you listened to them. There isn't much listening taking place in the market and if you can find someone supplying you their work who listens—and acts on what you say—you will have a great customer.

There is this caveat, however. If you make any commitment to the customer in these conversations—no matter how small, no matter how relevant to the job—you need to follow through on the commitment. Period.

Just as you are evaluating your new company, new manager, and new team for how well you can work with them, your customer is evaluating how well you will work with them. Blowing off a commitment from the first meeting is simply asking for a pained relationship with your customer. This means you need to record the commitment, track it, status it with your customer, and deliver it when you said you will get it done.

No exceptions.

Update Your Task System

At the beginning of this book, I talked about having your task management system updated and clean before starting on your new job. Now that we're in week four, you've used your task system to accomplish your work in your new job. If you are like most people, you are seeing some friction in that system. You are not capturing the right stuff to do, getting the follow-up system right or—worse—missing commitments.

Consequently, rather than just input tasks into your system and then do them as you work through the day, take some time to think through the entirety of the system. Are your tasks going into the right categories? How is that calendar working out on the new job? Are you capturing all of your commitments? Are you meeting all of your commitments?

Your task system is your friend—or your enemy

Everyone works differently when laying out a task system where they get something on a list and then work the list.

The saying about this is that you have to be attracted to your lists of tasks. You have to want to look at them and start right in on the next one. This is not easy. For almost everyone, there is some sort of resistance to adding to the lists, clarifying the lists, and working the lists.

For example, over the course of time I have discovered that I can't have much more than about ten items on a single list. Now, at any given time, I have 150–200 tasks on my various lists—and if you really captured *all* the commitments you have running around in your head, you would too.

But the deal is that if I have 20 items on a list, my eyes start to glaze over. I start wondering down the list and try and determine the priorities all over again. Pretty soon I'm checking e-mail and what is new on the Internet and before I know it, I'm totally out of a work zone.

For me, then, a key is to get the lists into manageable chunks where I can look at the list, easily figure out what is next and get moving on it.

The problem you have when you start a new job is that what was perfect organization and execution in your previous job will no longer be exactly the same on your new job. You may have to add a category or two so you can properly place tasks in them. Or you don't know what you don't know and you've put all those tasks into a single list because you didn't know how to categorize those tasks just yet. Your old job may have allowed you to scan your lists once a day but your new job changes so much that you need to scan the lists more often.

Your objective here, then, is to not use your task management system, but think about *how* you are using your task management system so you can find ways to improve it.

You've had four weeks now working on the new job and you should have experienced some irritation, glazed eyes, and resistance to some portions of your task management system. Now is the time to think through what was irritating you about how your system is set up, what was causing the glazed eyes, and look at those areas that you didn't want to look at.

You want to capture tasks, due dates, and anything else into the right categories so that you can sit down and start effortlessly knocking them off. If you have to pause and re-create the task before you can start working it, your task management system isn't where it needs to be for effective, productive work.

Now is the time to look at how your system is working and make updates to it to see if it removes drag on your work.

Update Your Cubicle

Your first week, you were given a space to do your work. If it was the typical office cubicle, you have some desk space, some desk drawer space and some overhead space. Perhaps you work best with nothing on your desk except your laptop or desktop computer and a phone. Or, perhaps, you work best with a hundred pictures on your desk of your family, friends, and adventure trips you have taken.

Regardless, when you got your space, you set it up how you thought it work best for you at the time.

Well, time has gone on and you are one month into the new job. Is that space still laid out so you are most productive? Are the filing systems you built working out for you? Is your overhead reference area doing the right job? Are those pictures coming in the way of getting your work done?

Let's examine plain old physical stuff. Is your chair in the most comfortable position? The right height? Can you talk on the phone and still access your computer or is that phone cord too short and too far away to work just right? Even something simple as the right kind of mouse that fits your hand can help your productivity and do wonders to protect against carpel tunnel syndrome. Simple changes? Yes. But the ergonomics in most cubicles are poor so we need to step back and examine our workspace.

Just like your task management system, how your cubicle is functioning for you can help you stay attracted to the work or irritate you all the time. At some point, because we set it up early, we decide to not change something in our cube until it gets so irritating we stop doing everything to fix the irritation.

My suggestion here is that this week you systematically review your workstation and determine what is working and not working about your space. Think through talking on the phone, meeting with people at your cube, working on your computer, writing your notes and attending conference calls. Think through how you file stuff and how you retrieve stuff you've filed.

As you go through these scenarios, you'll discover some things that need changing in your space. So change them. I've done something as simple as move the phone six inches in a different direction or gotten one of those snap in things to prevent the cord from tangling—and it took away what irritated me every time I picked up the phone.

Even if you notice one of these irritations and can't fix it right now, get it into your task lists so that you have captured the irritation. Then, when you do take the time here to think through your workspace, you will have some triggers to help you get your workspace to a better place to do your work.

If we're going to have a cube to do our work, let's make the cubicle serve our work needs to help us put forth our best work.

Weekly Review—Week Four

In this final, operational weekly review, you will want to focus on your customers. If you were able to ask the four questions of them, you should have learned a great deal about their needs, the benefits of your work, and how you can improve your work product.

As you review your customer notes, what common themes are you seeing? Always look for ways to improve what you do to deliver better output to your customers and, this early in the new job, make sure you are prototyping your work for your customer as well. This will help bring out hidden requirements that were not explained to you.

You should almost be able to set up "policies" for your customer. This customer wants the information this way and a different customer wants it provided a different way. Setting up these guidelines for delivery of your work to the customer based on your interactions with them helps you consistently deliver the exact work that your customer wants.

This is especially true of recurring work where you provide work consistently—say weekly—to customers. You want this recurring work to be consistently perfect because it reflects your commitment to customers. After all, if you don't do this, you can continually provide crappy work to your customers and you'll lose your "results" perception one delivery at a time.

Use this review to really get to the core of what great work means to your customer and set up ways to ensure you consistently provide great work. This includes your most important customer, your manager.

You took good, hard looks at your task system and workspace sometime during this week and made changes, right? So here at the weekly review, you may have some hints as to how those changes helped improve your workflow. Simply note them.

After this operational review—which I suggest you do every week on the job—you have one more review to do. You've been on your new job now for 30 days. Time to make some decisions.

7 Decision Points

How Long Will The Position Last?

At the end of 30 days on your new dream job, it is time for a reality check with a dose of perspective. Remember, jobs are two-way streets. Companies, specifically, your manager, need to know that you can deliver results to meet their work goals. Just as important, your new job needs to deliver what you needed when you set about going to get this job.

Before we started this 30-day marathon, I said that it was important for you to consider how long this new position will last. You came up with a time frame. Well, there is now much more you know about the job, the work, your team, manager, and customers than you knew walking into the job that first day.

So, now, how long do you think the job will last?

Knowing all that you know now, you come up with a time frame, say 18 months. How does that time frame match up with your original time frame? If it is different—and I am sure it is—why do you think the time frame is different, shorter or longer?

The answers to the "why the difference" question will reveal what you learned while on the job compared to when you were courted for the job. Does your new time frame result from new and cool things you learned in the last 30 days? Or does what you learn show promises made that never materialized? Is your team better than you thought at the beginning or is it hard to see how they could have ever been a team? Has your manager changed from the consultative person who thrives for new ideas from the team during the interview process to a "my way or the highway" decision-maker once he or she became your everyday manager?

The differences you see between your input before starting the job and now after being on the job offer great insight into how long a position will last. Keep monitoring how long you think a position will last—it is your great protection to ensure you start looking for a new job with enough time to control, as best you can, your income from your work.

Will the Position Match Your Goals?

Your second decision point is determining if your new job will deliver the goals you set for taking the job before you started.

Your goals for the job are important because they will help you determine if your work was worth it. Even if your only goal is to work at a company because of its name (think Google in the technology market or Epic in the health care market) and the notch on the resume it gives you, knowing your goals will help sustain you when times get tough. They will get tough, you know.

Now, after 30 days, how's that job matching up with the work goals you set for yourself before you started? Is this job going to help you reach them in the way you thought they could be reached? Or has the position been so great that you will get additional goals you didn't plan on from this job?

For the same reasons you want to compare and contrast how long a job lasts, you want to observe the differences in what you thought you could achieve with this job before you started to what you know now.

Doing so not only helps you determine if this job is right for you, it also can reveal a gap in your thinking about what you want out of a position that you can capture now for the next job search.

Where Can You Add Value?

Your third and final decision point is determining where you can best add unique value to your team, manager, and customers. Remember, doing what everyone else is doing puts your work on the track of commodity rather than a prized possession no one can do without. Having that unique value no one can live without won't protect you in most layoffs, but it can in some.

Regardless of the protection against layoffs, having this unique value translates into something that will have you remembered for the next position. Your goal here is to have people think that if they need "X," you are the person who can best provide it. That gets to your reputation on the job and is something to jealously guard as it becomes your personal brand.

You've spent a lot of time analyzing your manager, team and customers—where is that sweet spot of value you can uniquely bring to this situation? You should have had some good thoughts on that during week two and have had two more weeks to work to determine if the value you bring will work for you.

If there were more than one unique value you could bring to the team (and there should be), now is the time to decide to focus clearly on one or two of the values and really start to develop them. It's good for the manager, your team—and you.

You Rock!

Starting any new job is a kaleidoscope of new people, processes, and workspaces, and a fire hose of new information. Most people get past the kaleidoscope and get the fire hose settled down and then kick back, thinking they are doing well on the job.

They don't dig. They superficially evaluate the job based on what is on the tops of their heads.

If you have followed the practices in this book, you did a lot of digging. Plus, you structured the information to make sure that you acquired the maximum knowledge you could about the job, team, manager, stakeholders, and customers. As well, you increased your efficiency by reviewing your task management process and how your cubicle was set up for doing your work.

Most importantly, you worked to discover how long this position would last, set up and evaluated goals for the work and determined where you can best add value to the organization.

Very few people do this.

Following these practices is black belt career management for starting a new job. You will have significantly reduced the risk of failing on the job because you are focused on getting it quickly right with the people you work with and your customers. You will quickly know whether or not the job is right for you and meets your expectations. If it does, that's great. But if the job doesn't meet your expectations, you can work to change that or know early on that another job search is in your future.

Either way, the focus—correctly—is ensuring the work matches your needs, gives you an environment that provides satisfaction on the job, and helps the company reach their goals and yours. It puts you in a position of power because, unlike all the others simply going through the motions, you know what you want out of a job and can tell if you are getting it.

Congratulations on your success. You earned it.

About the Author

In our shifting economy, landing a job—any job—is a big deal. So if you land your *dream job*, you may find yourself so pleased and satisfied with your achievement that you think you're done. But, as *Scot Herrick* points out in *'I've Landed a Dream Job—Now What???'* to-day—more than ever before—you need to hit the ground running on day one of your new job.

Given current economics, having a new employ-ee get productive super fast is a huge advantage not only for the employee's manager but for the employee too. This can make the first 30 days at a new job intense and filled with anxiety because virtually everything is new—corporate culture, team dynamics, management styles, and more. It is difficult for you, as a new hire, to nail down what you know, who to ask, and which of your skills are most valued by your new organization.

Scot Herrick's purpose in writing this book is to help people like you, who have just landed a job at a large or small corporation, to get started on the right foot. Beginning with the often-overlooked basics, Scot shows you how to manage the transition from your old job, to evaluate the fit between your new workplace and yourself, to identify the real decision makers, to integrate into your new team's culture and, most important, to determine which aspects of your new role are most meaningful to your manager, and therefore most closely linked to your job security and paycheck.

'I've Landed a Dream Job—Now What???' is designed to be your constant companion during the first thirty days at your new job. It will help you think through what you're going to accomplish and how to measure your accomplishments, right from day 1 all the way to day 30. Weekly tasks and action items make sure you are on track and end-of-week reviews help you assess how closely you are meeting your goals. With Scot Herrick's book at your side, you can be sure to survive and thrive in your new cubicle.

Other Happy About® Books

Purchase these books at Happy About http://happyabout.info or at other online and physical bookstores.

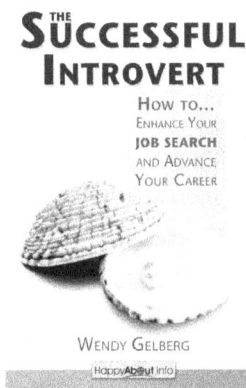

The Successful Introvert

SUCCESSFUL INTROVERT

How to...
Enhance Your
JOB SEARCH
and Advance
Your Career

Wendy Gelberg

HappyAbout info

The purpose of this book is to present strategies used by successful people—including numerous celebrities—in managing their introversion or shyness while becoming successful in professional endeavors.

Paperback: $19.95
eBook: $14.95

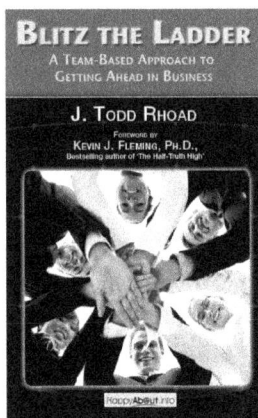

Blitz the Ladder

BLITZ THE LADDER
A Team-Based Approach to
Getting Ahead in Business

J. Todd Rhoad

Foreword by
Kevin J. Fleming, Ph.D.,
Bestselling author of 'The Half-Truth High'

HappyAbout info

The purpose behind publishing this book is to provide the many young professionals entering the business world a realistic view of how business is done and what they can expect to encounter.

Paperback: $19.95
eBook: $14.95

SECOND EDITION I'M ON LINKEDIN
Now What???

JASON ALBA
FOREWORD BY BOB BURG

HappyAbout Info

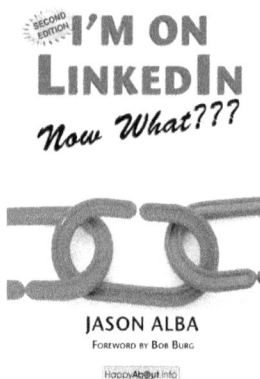

Networking Online—Making LinkedIn Work for you!

This book explains the benefits of using LinkedIn and recommends best practices so that you can get the most out of it.

Paperback: $19.95
eBook: $14.95

STORYTELLING ABOUT YOUR BRAND
Online & Offline

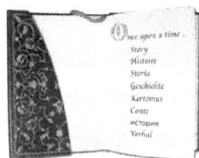

BERNADETTE MARTIN
FOREWORD BY WILLIAM ARRUDA
AFTERWORD BY JASON ALBA

Happy About

Storytelling About Your Brand Online & Offline

This book covers the gamut of online and offline opportunities available to tell the story about the "Brand Called You" to your target audience in a compelling way.

Paperback: $22.95
eBook: $16.95

CPSIA information can be obtained
at www.ICGtesting.com
Printed in the USA
LVHW081122070321
680806LV00016B/433